D1461730

Submitted in partial fulfilment of
the requirements of
Leeds Metropolitan Unversity
for the award of the degree of
Doctor of Philosophy
on the basis of published work.

July, 2000

Imagination, Identification and Catharsis
in Theatre and Therapy

of related interest

The Glass of Heaven
The Faith of the Dramatherapist
Roger Grainger
ISBN 1 85302 284 5

Drama and Healing
The Roots of Drama Therapy
Roger Grainger
ISBN 1 85302 337 X

**Dramatherapy with Families,
Groups and Individuals**
Waiting in the Wings
Sue Jennings
ISBN 1 85302 014 1 hb
ISBN 1 85302 144 X pb

Art Therapy and Dramatherapy
Masks of the Soul
Sue Jennings and Åse Minde
ISBN 1 85302 027 3 hb
ISBN 1 85302 181 4 pb

**Storymaking in Education and
Therapy**
Alida Gersie and Nancy King
ISBN 1 85302 519 4 hb
ISBN 1 85302 520 8 pb

Storymaking in Bereavement
Dragons Fight in the Meadow
Alida Gersie
ISBN 1 85302 065 6 hb
ISBN 1 85302 176 8 pb

**Reflections on Therapeutic
Storymaking**
Alida Gersie
ISBN 1 85302 272 1

**Dramatic Approaches to Brief
Therapy**
Edited by Alida Gersie
ISBN 1 85302 271 3

Persona and Performance
The Meaning of Role in Drama,
Therapy and Everyday Life
Robert J Landy
ISBN 1 85302 229 2 hb
ISBN 1 85302 230 6 pb

Essays in Drama Therapy
The Double Life
Robert J Landy
ISBN 1 85302 322 1

Dramatherapy
Clinical Studies
Edited by Steve Mitchell
ISBN 1 85302 304 3

Play Therapy
Where the Sky Meets the Underworld
Ann Cattanach
ISBN 1 85302 211 X

Play Therapy with Abused Children
Ann Cattanach
ISBN 1 85302 193 8

Children's Stories in Play Therapy
Ann Cattanach
ISBN 1 85302 362 0

Imagination, Identification and Catharsis in Theatre and Therapy

Mary Duggan and Roger Grainger

Jessica Kingsley Publishers
London and Bristol, Pennsylvania

First published in the United Kingdom in 1997 by
Jessica Kingsley Publishers Ltd
116 Pentonville Road
London N1 9JB, England
and
1900 Frost Road, Suite 101
Bristol, PA 19007, U S A

Copyright © 1997 Mary Duggan and Roger Grainger

Library of Congress Cataloging in Publication Data

A CIP catalogue record for this book is available from the Library of Congress

British Library Cataloguing in Publication Data

A CIP catalogue record for this book is available from the British Library

ISBN 1 85302 431 7

Printed and Bound in Great Britain by
Athenaeum Press, Gateshead, Tyne and Wear

Contents

Acknowledgements

We would like to thank the following who have helped us, in one way or another, to write this book. First of all, our fellow dramatherapists: Madeleine Andersen-Warren, John Casson, Judy Donovan, Alida Gersie, Marina Jenkyns, Sue Jennings, David Powley and Ted Wharam.

Next, those in the theatre itself, notably Peter Cheeseman, Clare Higgins, Joan Littlewood, Hugh Miller, Brian Wilde.

We would like to thank Miller Mair for kind permission to quote from 'Between Psychology and Psychotherapy'.

We gratefully acknowledge support given by the Wakefield and Pontefract Community NHS Trust, and particularly, by members of the various dramatherapy groups involved with us in our voyage of exploration and discovery.

We are indebted to the support of all those people; but we would like to make the point that without the enthusiasm and long-suffering of Gerard, Aidan and Doreen, we could not have written more than the first few pages.

For Kate and Mungo Duggan

Can I see another's woe
And not be in sorrow too,
Can I see another's grief
And not seek for kind relief

Can I see a falling tear
And not feel my sorrow's share?

William Blake
(*Songs of Innocence*)

Maturity is the capacity to move in and out of dramatic reality when appropriate.

Sue Emmy Jennings
(1996)

Introduction

It is a Friday morning. I arrive at the Education centre, tired after a busy week, but ready to run a workshop to introduce a group of health professionals to some of the ideas of dramatherapy. Entering the room, I am underwhelmed by a sense of indifference from the group. I remind myself that it is Friday, and they are probably tired too. I help myself to a cup of coffee, and before I have a chance to take even one sip, one of the women turns towards me. 'I think that it's only fair to tell you' she begins 'that most of us are sceptical about this dramatherapy stuff'. My heart sinks. When you are dealt an unpromising hand in poker, the sensible thing to do is to stack; to put down your cards without playing them, and wait for a better hand. I am strongly tempted to stack at this point. I would like to think that it was my professionalism that kept me going, but I suspect that a healthy streak of cowardice actually prevented me from giving in on the spot. 'That's OK' I reply 'I am interested in where that scepticism is coming from. I wonder if you know?' 'Well,' she says 'some of us watched a programme the other night that showed some dramatherapy, and we all felt that it was…that the whole thing was basically false'. I pause for thought. Nothing comes. Suddenly, my mouth knows what it wants to say, even though my brain doesn't. 'Of course it was false. How could it not be?' Everyone is watching and listening now. This evident capitulation right at the start takes them by surprise. They are ready to listen. 'But let me ask you' I continue 'how many of you have been to see a really good film recently?' People's faces begin to light up as they recall seeing a recently released tear-jerker, or other films that have moved them in some way. 'Right. Each one of you has seen at least one film that provoked a strong emotional response. But that film wasn't "real" any more than a dramatherapy session is "real". In fact it is a lot less real. However, you responded to the film *as if* it were really happening. That is dramatic reality. For sure, dramatic reality is not the same as actuality, but in terms of therapy, that is the whole point. Dramatic reality is a special and safe form of reality where we can begin to make experiments.'

It is easy, and even seems logical to dismiss the concept of dramatic reality as a paradox, a contradiction in terms. How can a dramatic act have reality, when it is patently unreal, in the sense that it is a presentation of events which have not actually happened, or a representation of the past. Yet each one of us has experienced that reality, has engaged sufficiently with the drama to produce within ourselves some kind of emotional response. We have responded 'as if' what we witness is actually happening. What occurs here is created by both the actor and the spectator: Grotowski's definition of theatre is 'what takes place between actor and spectator' (1975, 32). It is a subtle and unvoiced contract between the two, based on the actor's skill and the spectator's openness to the dramatic experience: we will act and respond as if these things are so. It is necessarily an act of sharing. The actor shares with the audience the 'gift of the self' which is the act of total self-exposure which transcends the barrier between them. When actors and audience are thus joined in the shared drama, then dramatic reality is created, and a central part of this reality is the concept of 'as if'; the reaction to a set of given circumstances 'as if' they were so.

This book is mainly concerned with dramatic impersonation. However, the phrase 'as if' signifies more than 'pretending to be someone else', or even 'imagining something or someone to be different from how I first perceived them', In fact, of course, it denotes a principle basic to humanness itself, that of *freedom or flexibility of thought, and therefore of experience.* The dictionary definition of *as if* is 'as the case would be'. It is entirely feasible for us to imagine a state of affairs in which the case could not be any different from what it actually is. Human beings, however, do not usually think like this, and there is evidence to suggest that they find it hard to do so, unless they are clinically depressed: 'If ifs and an's were pots and pans, we would all of us be tinkers.'

The social psychologist Erving Goffman (1961, 131ff) made a vitally important contribution to our understanding of human relationships, particularly in his concept of 'role-distance'. This refers to our manipulation of the ways in which we present ourselves to other people. We are able to adopt the most suitable role for our present purpose, whatever this may be. The distance consists in our freedom to choose an appropriate 'self'. If we only had one social role we would have no room for manoeuvre. The words 'present', 'role', even 'distance', suggest a state of affairs in which we actively choose among various ways of participating in relationships with other people – and perhaps, too, with ourselves. We are not entirely free to do this, of course, because of the pressure put on us by our social circumstances to take on roles that other people would prefer to see us playing. In the final analysis, our humanity is expressed in freedom to choose and responsibility for choosing. We should not let Goffman's use of language taken from the world of theatre mislead us into underestimating the seriousness of his purpose or the appropriateness of his imagery in expressing it. Theatre, like life, is a serious business, even though it chooses, on occasion, to present itself as 'mere entertainment'. This, in fact, is the source of the ability to convince us, as it communicates unexpected understandings that come upon us from beyond ourselves and expand our awareness by calling forth an unrehearsed response. 'Entertain imagination of a time...' Shakespeare's Prologue says in *Henry V*, and Goffman points out that despite sociological assumptions, the phenomenon of 'role distance' demonstrates that we are not confined by the particular roles we play. One thing remains true; because we are people the most significant factors in our environment are other people, their actions and intentions, or even their simple existence, so that by 'social interaction' we really mean relationship. It is relationship that demands space, schematic or concrete, because *space between-ness* is what defines the relationship of subject and object, who am I or what, or who, the other is.

As we shall see, the principles of theatre's use of 'as if' are those of 'separation and contact', 'safety and danger', and 'dispersed attention and focus'. These are really descriptions of psychological dimensions, what the cognitive psychologist George Kelly (1955, 199) calls 'constructs': ways of assessing the personal value of our experience of reality. We devise our own worlds so as not to be surprised by what we may find there – which is why we have to keep changing them.[1] Constructs resemble the 'frames of reality' described by Goffman, in that they refer not only to values but to different kinds of values: we use them to distinguish quality as well as quantity, ranking them in order of complete dimensions from less significant (from the point of view of our meaning system) to most significant, concerned with life's essential meaning. The three dimensions of 'as if' mentioned above all refer to the central pole of a construct system, the backbone of an attitude to life itself. The thing that comes home to us when we look at these three

---

1   'A construct is like a reference axis, a basic dimension of appraisal, often unverbalised, frequently unsymbolised, and occasionally unsignified in any manner save by the elemental processes it governs... A construct is a way in which two or more things are alike and *thereby* different from a third or more things.' (Kelly, G. 1955, 199)

dimensions in terms of the value systems supported and inspired by them, is that they all express the same understanding. All involve the degree of difference in separation between self and other. All three dimensions are different aspects of the same existential gesture and of the responsiveness evoked by it, in which we move outward from ourselves to a source of being which is not us and live, albeit momentarily, *as if it were.* Separation, safety, dispersed attention all obviously belong together: because we are separated from either the presence or idea of danger, we need never engage all the powers of our being towards a single source or object.

The principle of focus is crucial here, because it precedes the possibility of any kind of engagement with anything at all, either 'inside' or 'outside' the self. Here again, however, the tension which joins the two poles of the construct is irresistible: it is the actual presence of what is calling me to abandon separateness/safety/inattentiveness that draws me out of myself and sets me voyaging.

The underlying principle, then, is this: from the security given by love, love that is 'good enough', comes the serenity to turn outwards towards the other, to give oneself away in love, and to play a role in regard to another in the freedom of loving. Personification – the bestowal of selfhood on someone else out of the security of one's own self-being – and role are interdependent: both refer to the image of self-in-relation. Personification and impersonation go together in human social experience, as we both give being to and receive it from one another. From the very beginning of our awareness of others, we are aware of their awareness of us; indeed, according to Lacan (1977), we actually project that awareness upon them, as the mirror-image of our own perceiving. Human understanding is always a reflected awareness.

As G.H. Mead (1967, 141) wrote: 'The specifically social expressions of intelligence…depend on the given individual's ability to take the roles of, or put himself in the place of the other individuals implicated with him in given social situations.' Similarly, Charles Cooley spoke of 'The looking-glass self'. This was in 1922; nearly 50 years later, Mary Hamilton (1986, 93) reminds us that 'metacognition' – the ability to draw conclusions about things that do not directly involve the self – is facilitated by social interaction. The interplay of social roles is not just a game in which we find a use for our native ingenuity. It is, in a very real sense, *ourselves.* The fact is, I must know how you see me in order to be me at all. My own personification depends on an impersonation, not necessarily of you, but of *your ideas and expectations of me.*

Mead's original formulation about the reflexivity of human awareness involved consciousness of a single 'I' and a multiplicity of 'me's', corresponding to myself as I see others seeing me: 'We divide ourselves up in all sorts of different selves with reference to our acquaintances' (Mead, 142). Not only with regard to them, but in our own eyes too. Roles can be intra-personal, in the sense that we see them corresponding to different aspects of ourself, as well as inter-personal, referring to other people. Many psychological difficulties are traceable to internal role-conflicts in which one of the personages in our interior drama is locked in conflict with another (Mair, 1977). As Moreno pointed out, these are the intrapersonal comedies and tragedies out of which we construct our public self-presentation to the world of other people, and to ourselves as members of that world. It is in terms of, and as a result of such dramas that our individual personalities develop (Fox, 1987).

In everything we do, we stand out from ourselves in order to focus upon the other, and upon ourselves-as-other. The perpetual movement out-and-back-and-out-again is the source and substance of our lives as persons, the action that constitutes our world. Our understanding is characteristically at a distance, as we try to find clues as to the plot of the drama in which we are currently and chronically involved, by acting 'as if' we were in fact two people, not one—one involved, the other detached and calmly observing the social scene... As we shall see, there is more to human social experience than awareness of role-structure, and more to theatre than its demonstration in dramatic form.

CHAPTER 1

As If and Identification

In the language of psychology, 'as if' stands for the way of thinking and behaving whereby I imagine that I am you and you me: in other words, that we have become the same person. This is certainly a major proposal, and we are certainly indebted to the imagination for the ability to entertain it. To imagine that you are 'in the place of' somebody else, and that what is happening to them is happening to you, is to turn towards them with a gesture which must, to be realistic and convincing, include the whole self – yours and theirs. The as if of people requires no less than that a person imagine him or herself turning to someone body and soul. This image is total and allows no remainder. As if lies at the heart of human relationship, a kind of limiting case.

Thus, to consider relationship in terms that are fully human we must draw near to people themselves rather than to psychological 'mechanisms' of any kind. Faced with so profound a mystery as human relationship we are forced to widen our epistemological horizons to take in more than social and cognitive psychology are able – or willing – to envisage. According to the existential anthropology of Martin Buber (1966), it is the separation between self and other, 'I and Thou', which permits the relationship of persons.[1] The ultimate meaning of our existence consists not in oneself or in the other person but in what happens between us. Buber describes an alternating awareness in which the other living beings, whether they are animal, human or divine are experienced successively as subject and object. This may be expressed in various ways in order to be understood. The suggestion is that the human consciousness loses its separate identity in the moment of

---

1   cf. Derrida, J., *Writing and Difference*, trans. A. Bass, (London, Routledge, 1978) 'The other is absolutely other only if he is an ego, that is, in a certain way, if he is the same as I' (p.127). He speaks of 'The being-together as separation which precedes and exceeds society' (p.95).

encounter with whatever is not itself, but immediately withdraws from the other so that it may interiorise and 'understand' what has just happened before venturing forth to repeat the process. Obviously this requires some kind of space between persons, otherwise the movements involved cannot be imagined as taking place. Buber sees the interaction in existential terms, as the gesture of I towards Thou which is so personal, so much a gift of the whole self, that it cannot be sustained without immediately returning to itself – otherwise I would cease to be a person and so would you, for we would immediately lose our own individuality in the self-hood of the other. On the other hand, it is in the gift of self to other, the reciprocal gesture in which we address 'the being that is not I' that our own personhood subsists. Both existential positions, I–Thou – in which I encounter the other, and I–It – in which I withdraw to draw my own conclusions about the encounter, belong together and are aspects of the one relational gesture. Nevertheless the meaning of the gesture resides as certainly in their separateness which allows them perpetually to unite, and thus to know what the union of individual selves actually means. The gesture itself is a tension, located, poetically speaking, in the space between Thou and It, which both separates and unites, and is in itself a union of separatenesses, preserved from undifferentiated union or total independence by the interchange between them. The entire image is of a structure which provides freedom and spontaneity within itself: 'Without "It" man cannot live – But he who lives with "It" alone is not a man' (1966: 34).

In works of art this metaphorical structure, the poetic 'space for encounter', becomes a visible, tactile, aural, olfactory presence or sensory experience. Works of art are particularly precious because they are symbols of encounter, and as such, encourage and permit the relationship of persons. This is because, of the two primary words of existence, It and Thou, only the former may be externalised; the work of art is the concretisation of part of a living relation that may be grasped by the senses. This is the word that cannot itself produce life, but is able nonetheless to locate it; the 'eternal chrysalis' to which Thou is the 'eternal butterfly' (Buber, 1966, 17). In a remarkable passage Buber (9, 10) describes the process of artistic creation as follows:

> A man is faced by a form which desires to be made by him into a work. This form is no offspring of his souls, but is an appearance which steps up to it and demands of it the effective power. The man is concerned with an act of his being. If he carries it through, if he speaks the primary word ['Thou' that is] out of his being to the form which appears, then the effective power streams out and the work arises... The work produced is a thing among things, able to be

experienced and described as a sum of qualities. But from time to time it can face the receptive beholder in its whole embodied form...

In other words, it encounters us 'as if' it were alive, reaching out to us in relationship and permitting all who come into contact with it to live in relationship with one another.

Works of art, then, clear a space around the known and understood for what is not yet incorporated in the ranks of our formulated experience of the world. The image of Thou and It is itself such a work, as are the two models of Goffman's social theatre and Kelly's route-map for personal journeys. Relationship is here seen as a dance, experienced as most perfectly co-ordinated when the dancers are furthest apart. Each of these is a metaphor for the self's experience of the other, and of the self that experiences the other, approached as if it were something else, something sensible and memorable, the right shape for drawing conclusions. Metaphors, mental images, conventional signs – both linguistic and numerical – psychological symbols, all serve as tools for relating to and accommodating (in Piaget's sense of including within the cognitive system) what is not the self but must be taken into account by the self in coming to personal terms with the world and with life.

This is vital for our understanding of the significance of what we have referred to as 'as if'. We must be aware, first of all, of our separateness from the world in order to make any kind of practical, creative sense of it – or, in other words, to get on with the business of living. Observation and analysis of childhood experience suggest that we do not have such a sense from the beginning: it is something that we have each one of us to learn for him or herself – and the learning is always a painful process. D.W. Winnicott (1988, 8), one of the founder members of Object Relations Theory, describes it as follows:

> First, from a primary merging of the individual with the environment, comes an emergence, the individual staking a claim, being able to be in a world that is *dis*claimed; then the strengthening of the self as an entity, a continuity of being as a place where, and from where, the self as a unit, as something body-bound and dependent on physical care emerges; and then the dawning awareness (and awareness implies the existence of mind) of dependence, and of the mother's dependability and of her love, which comes through to the infant as physical care and close adaptation to need.

Thus Winnicott sees the emergence of our awareness of *something beside ourself* in terms of a consciousness of *interdependence* rather than opposition or rivalry

– although these things too begin to play a part in the moulding of the individual personality. The quality of nurture that we receive certainly affects our eventual ability to accept one another as persons, and to trust in the goodwill of people other than ourselves. It also provides a safe environment for the expression of frustrated resentment when we do not immediately receive the satisfaction to which we have grown accustomed. In these first weeks and months at the breast we begin to discover both the positive and negative implications of life with other people, its opportunities for loving and hating, accepting and rejecting what is around us.

Object relations theory concerned the growth of the capacity for be-tween-ness in human beings. Freud (1953, 122) uses the word 'object' to refer to 'the thing in regard to which, or through which, the instinct is able to achieve its aim.' Object relations, however, proposes a view of psychic structures in which persons are drawn into contact with each other by the personal need for relationships rather than being, as Freud maintained, driven into conflict with one another by the forces of impersonal instinct (Fairbairn, 1952, 59-81). The first object, then, is the mother's breast. During the initial months of life libidinal satisfaction is not perceived as existing apart from the self. There is no need at this point to imagine that the breast is there when it is absent; it is always there, whenever it is needed. With the need to comfort oneself when actual succour is not available – when, prior to weaning, the breast is not given so often and the baby must get used to waiting for longer periods, so that he or she becomes aware of not being in total control of the situation – the need for some kind of fantasy satisfaction arises. Melanie Klein describes how 'the baby's impulses and feelings are accompanied by a kind of mental activity which I take to be the most primitive one: that is phantasy building, or more colloquially, imaginative thinking' (1937, in 1988; 308).[2] The child desires comfort from the image of the breast and of the satisfaction, emotional as well as physical – or rather *because of* physical – that it represents. 'Such primitive phantasying is the earliest form of the capacity which later develops into the more elaborate workings of the imagination' (Klein, 1988, 308). This is the beginning of the power to experiment with alternative states of affairs in order to escape to some extent from the demands and limitations of the present situation. In other words, it is the origin of 'as if' itself. Winnicott (1971, 6) points out that 'When symbolism is employed the infant is already clearly distinguish-ing between fantasy and fact, between inner and external events'. He goes

---

2 Generally speaking, 'phantasy' is used to mean an intra-psychic structure, and 'fantasy', a conscious inter-personal mode of communication.

on to say that such an awareness is essential in order to function as a healthy human being ('The inability to make any links between inner and outer worlds is seen in its full malignancy' in schizophrenic breakdown).

In order to do this, however, a child must have a certain self-confidence, a robust sense of its own being. *To be as oneself* must precede *existing as distinct from something, or someone else.* This self-confidence is not innate, although of course the potential for it must come into the world with the child. It takes considerably longer for us to stand on our own two feet emotionally than it does physically, and the first process begins before the second. When we see a small child stumbling about in the area we have specifically cleared for her on the living room floor, continually falling over, tripping over her own feet, we may reflect that she has had considerable practice in experimentation, and will go on experimenting with relationships long after ceasing to be a toddler. In the first place, room for this kind of development is provided by the 'benign circle' of the mother's 'extremely delicate adaptation to the emotional needs of the infant' (Winnicot, 1988, 101), permitting the illusion of total autonomy that a child must have in order to complete his journey away from the maternal womb and the stage of primary identification with mother and find his feet in a world full of other people, all of whom are engaged in the same struggle for self-expression, the vast majority of them having had considerably more practice!

A vital stage in the development of self-consciousness is the discovery of the negative emotions of guilt and fear. As satisfaction becomes less automatic, less an integral part of the self, the impulse to cling on to it, to use force to wrest it from the mother's breast emerges ever more forcefully. With it comes the anxiousness of running the risk of alienating the source of sustenance and 'killing the goose that lays the golden eggs'. Melanie Klein speaks of this as the 'depressive position'. This refers not to actual emotional illness but to the vital developmental stage at which a child becomes aware for the first time that its own impulses may in fact interfere with its relationship with its mother. This is extremely important because it is from such an unpromising start – the awareness of responsibility for pain in another person – that the capacity to moderate one's impulses out of consideration for someone else proceeds; and this, of course, is the basis of a loving relationship (Winnicot, 1988, 69–83). We learn to see another person as themselves, rather than as a dangerous split-off part of ourselves.[3]

---

3   cf. also J. Lacan, 1977. Lacan maintains that the child emerges from the condition of total unwilled identification with its mother by going through a *mirror* stage of psychological development, in which it starts to see itself and its mother, and eventually other people, as independent selves, capable of hurting and being themselves hurt. It

These are the contradictory feelings that children have to struggle with during the period when they are being weaned. They need two things: love and permission to experiment with the world that is opening up around them. The two things hang together, the second being, at this stage, the most appropriate and effective form of the first, as it encourages the growing child to use the way that he or she feels about the world in order to construct a model or picture of her or himself that may be lived with and further developed. This is the freedom to engage with otherness by negotiation in terms of one's own existence. It is very different from freedom to escape into oneself and find refuge in private fantasy, although, in order for it to be freedom, both options must be open. The result of what Winnicott calls 'good enough' mothering is that most of the time the child is encouraged to choose the first rather than the second (1971, 71, 15).

The choice is expressed behaviourally in actions undertaken in and toward the world, rather than invisibly as a simple change in mental attitudes. The change occurs when metaphor takes over from fantasy. The first is an alternative to the reality of the world of personal relationships, whereas the second employs the imagination to expand that world, making absent things present by attributing metaphysical significance to ordinary objects and experiences and giving concrete shape to abstract meaning. To this extent, metaphors are meeting places in which the transpersonal, transtemporal significance of things that happen in human life become attached to certain key images drawn from ordinary everyday experience. As in Martin Buber's model of human truth, metaphor is meaning that oscillates between presence and distance, possibility and impossibility, what is familiar and what cannot be immediately grasped. Both poles are experiential and concern human awareness; but what is signified owes its place in human discourse to its relationship with a category that is immediately apparent, an ordinary part of the human environment. Winnicott describes the action of transforming the open-endedness of abstract ideas like freedom and independence into the immediacy of here and now experience by providing the emerging personhood of a growing child with what he calls 'potential space' – an actual play area in which she can really be free and (relatively) independent, and which will come to mean these things to her over the days and weeks that she will spend playing there. As a concept, 'potential space' refers to a kind of psychological event, intervening between fantasy and reality; it is

---

is at this vital stage that sympathy with someone else emerges, and we can 'weep with those who weep'. Without the development of this kind of awareness, of course, the Oedipal scenario would make no real sense. (For a careful analysis of the nature of dramatic identification, see Jones, 1991.)

difficult to dwell on the idea without becoming conscious of its actual, *usable presence* – which of course is the way that the child knows it.

During every period of human life, playing is of the very greatest importance to us. In *The Art of Play*, Adam and Alée Blatner (1988) comment on the significance for all genuinely human experience of 'the special category of playfulness. This is a condition of social interaction in which behavior doesn't carry the same meaning as it might in the "ordinary" or non-play state of experience.' In this paradoxical state of mind things are 'real and not real at the same time. The mind seems to experience a kind of pleasure in being able to encompass these seemingly irreconcilable opposites' (Blatner and Blatner, 1988, 29). It is an enjoyable awareness, as it serves to relieve two kinds of anxiety at once. In games our experience of other people is both profounder and more trivial than it is in the real world. The imaginatively constructed world of the game provides us with responsibilities we can bear and possibilities we can exploit within the sphere of inter-personal experience. Games nourish our enjoyment of other people, while exorcising our fear of them. The fear belongs to our vulnerability. Because it is only a game we don't feel so exposed; because the experience of meeting and sharing that it provides is an authentic one, it gives us confidence and makes us feel real. This 'playing with danger and safety' will be a major theme of what follows. Because it is characteristic of the way in which we learn to regard ourselves in the presence of others, it is fundamental to the way that drama and theatre work.

Blatner and Blatner suggest that in games and playing our minds delight in experimenting with our sense of personal identity for the satisfaction we derive from it. 'It seems the mind finds pleasure in manipulating its own inconsistencies – the process gives some mastery over confusion, allows the imagination to expand and extends the sense of identity to include a greater range of experience.'[4] Games of hide and seek, in which Mother hides and Baby goes through the motions of trying to find her, serve a dual function of establishing 'object constancy' – the ability to cope with someone's absence without jumping to the conclusion that they have gone for ever, and will never return – and internalising the experience of loss and restoration as a kind of pleasant psychological trick whereby pseudo-anxiety can be

---

4   Blatner, A. & Blatner, A., *op. cit.*, 30. The importance of playing for human growth and development is stressed: 'In play, children and adults experience a holistic integration of many components of learning: spontaneous originality, emotional reactions, unconscious motivations, personal temperament and style, social and cultural context, as well as more researched intellectual processes. Play…is a primal form of learning by doing' (p.34). See also Erikson, 1965.

invoked in order to enjoy real emotional relief. Here again, the theatrical implications are obvious!

This kind of delight at being able to control one's emotional reactions doesn't come automatically. Before a game can be enjoyed, we must be sure that it its only a game, and consequently harmless. Gregory Bateson (1973) draws attention to the way in which this information is usually transmitted. It is done by means of what he calls 'meta-communication': communication about communication. We let one another know that what we are going to do or say next is not to be taken seriously, at 'face value': or rather, that it *is* to be taken seriously *as a game*, in which the underlying seriousness of the intention is being brought to our attention by being presented in a special way. Some of these games can be very serious indeed!

A metacommunicative gesture involves verbal or non-verbal signals as to the kind of social frame (to use Goffman's term) in which the ensuing exchange of meaning should be understood to be taking place. Even before we are able to find the right words, we have all kinds of ways of communicating information. We can do it solemnly or light-heartedly, to tease or convince, revealing our intentions or disguising them, in order to be taken seriously or simply to enjoy fooling about with an idea or situation. In fact, human beings commonly communicate with one another on several levels at once, using various kinds of signal – verbal, postural, kinetic; by tone of voice and quality of inflection as well as the specific choice of words and phrases; by facial expression and direction of gaze or level of glance; by choice of linguistic context or the use of jargon, or special 'private' languages, according to the custom of lovers or mothers talking to their babies. As we grow to maturity, we become more and more skilful at ringing the changes. We shift rapidly from one kind of message, requiring its own kind of interpretation, to another which follows a completely different set of rules. We metacommunicate simultaneously on several levels, enjoying the mental exercise involved. Theatre exploits our skill in changing from one kind of knowing to another. From this point of view, experimenting with ways of presenting information is what theatre is about. The name of the game is metacommunication.

But we must always be aware that it *is* a game. Under certain circumstances our juggling with so many different kinds of message only causes confusion and the breakdown of communication altogether. The burden of communication rests not only on what is said, but how it is said. This means that the two strands are of equal importance, but because one is to be seen in the light of the other it is essential they should be distinguishable as message and metamessage. If they are both received as having the same value as straightforward representations of intended meanings they simply register as self-contradiction and communicative chaos. The 'double bind' theory of the causation of schizophrenia proposes just such a process occurring in the way that some parents express their attitudes towards, and expectations of, the children who look toward them for validation of their efforts to make sense of the confusing world of childhood.

Drama and theatre provide examples of the interplay of message and metamessage in human social behaviour, giving us the opportunity to stand back and take notice of the subtle ways in which people like the ones we know (like ourselves, in fact) manage to get their real meanings across to one another, or effectively deceive one another, or arrive at compromises between these two positions which suit their own particular purposes. More funda-mentally, theatre and drama, by the fact that they admit to being a particular way of looking at life, *and include this admission in the statement they make about human reality*, assert the epistemological importance of the difference between communication and metacommunication. The message of drama itself is quite simply this, that we should look on this game *as if* it were reality. This, of course, is the message of all true games.

It is obvious, then, that to understand drama and theatre at all, we must first understand the business of playing itself. 'Business' is a good word to use: when we play, we are preoccupied with our own fantasy. This is not necessarily private. Indeed, from quite early on – perhaps as soon as we become aware of another person as *another* – we are willing to share our fantasy with them, to involve them in our inventions and become involved in theirs. Drama originates in reciprocal fantasy. First of all, however, we must be able to play by ourselves, in our own world on images, enjoying our own creations.

For this we need space. To the growing child the actual, physical, geographic location which gives him room to play by himself, and the time allowed to create imaginatively without continually being interrupted or deflected from his task are associated with the action whereby he or she enters a world of fantasy which will always be available, always ready waiting. Playtime and playspace are the laboratory for image making and image sharing, the terms on which we realise a new social world by exteriorising the inner fantasies which until now have preoccupied our developing awareness. Winnicot describes how, within the space for playing, the child experiments with fantasy in an entirely new way – fantasies that have been given permission to exist and so, within these circumstances, to assume the forms of reality. It is here that ideas assume the shape of actions and actions the scope of ideas. The growing child experiments with 'transitional objects', things which stand instead of something else and yet somehow participate in what they signify – in other words, toys. Toys are both aggressive and defensive. They attempt to control the threatening otherness of the world by reproducing it in safe, accommodatable versions, nursery forms that keep the real thing at bay while taking on some of its characteristics. In this toys perform much the same function as works of art, which both draw form from and impose form upon life. Whether it be a toy or a work of art (or indeed a theory or a formula, a doctrine or a system); or whether it takes on a theoretical or concrete existence, the transitional object serves as a link between subject and object, object and subject. The symbol points away from itself in two directions, as it signifies both an entire class of things like itself and also the metaphorical meaning of the class. The child who is experimenting with a piece of wood that has suddenly become interpretable as a gun is more conscious of the first kind of symbolism, 'class' or 'type' symbolism, but the exercise is stored up in his memory to be used whenever he needs to draw on ideas of killing or death or imagines himself defending somebody he loves who is in danger.

The object itself may stand for a person, of course. Winnicott is concerned to show how personal objects play the key role in changing private fantasy into the kind of imagination which allows us to take up a position, metaphorically speaking, in the lives of others who are not ourselves. 'This area of playing is not inner psychic reality. It is outside the individual, but it is not in the external world – the child gathers objects or phenomena from external reality and uses them in the service of some sample derived from inner or personal reality' (1971, 51).[5] In one sense, of course, everything is in the external world, as the child plays with his toys in the safe area set aside for such activity. In another sense, what matters from the point of view of the development of our ability to form personal relationships is an interior shift, as we discover a way of reaching out from ourselves and encountering someone else without either being destroyed by them or, what is equally terrifying, actually destroying them. Transitional objects arise out of our reaction to the fear that we have noted with regard to the depressive position. Feelings which might harm or even destroy Mother, and lay waste the entire world, are seen to leave her unscathed when I let whatever it may be that has

---

5   Winnicot's idea fits in with the notion put forward by Geza Roheim, that society itself is 'knitted together by projection of primary introjected objects or concepts followed by a series of subsequent introjections and projections' (*The Origin and Function of Culture*, New York; Nervous and Mental Disease Monographs, 1943:82). Society affords human nature that protection against its own impulses and the environmental hazards surrounding it which it must have as (in Nietzsche's phrase) 'a not-yet determined animal'.

taken on her identity stand in her place. My anger is no longer able to destroy the love that sustains me, and can take its place in the various emotions which I can allow myself to feel towards other people. Because it combines danger and safety, imaginative play is the key to human relationships, functioning as a link between personal realities, leading us across into participation with what is not ourselves and then back again, externalising the inner exchange which is the poetic reality of that relationship.

'As if' is the determining condition for, and the primary purpose of, every transitional object. Toys, plays, symphonies; wedding rings, academic hoods, membership certificates; stages, arenas, acting areas of every kind, formal or improvised – all are objects of and for transition. 'As if' is the experimental gambit on which an appreciation of the reality of otherness – difference from myself – depends. Its importance in the development of individual people cannot be overestimated. The alliances which as social beings we must form among ourselves depend on the ability to differentiate, because without an awareness of difference there can be no recognition of commonality. Seeing someone else as if they were I, rather than simply part of me, requires the ability to see myself as if I were them. The psychoanalytic account of relationship centres around a situation of social rivalry, in which a child recognises his or her same-sex parent as a rival for possession of the parent of the opposite sex. In order for such a situation to arise the growing child must be well aware that his or her rival possesses the same desires as she or he does, and is in a position to take punitive action if they are thwarted. Tension is relieved by the growth of awareness that, not only is the rival parent like the erring – or potentially erring – child, but the child is sufficiently like the parent, at least in this matter, that he or she may associate him or herself with the parent's attitudes and motives.

Thus instead of assuming the dangerous role of competitor, the post-Oedipal child develops within her- or himself the characteristics that will build up an alliance with the parent whose gender identity is shared. In such a way, we learn to identify with those whose characteristics, role and life-situation is like our own. It is important to notice that it involves more than a single change of direction. In fact, it is a developmental process taking place within a particular inter-personal situation, a set of circumstances arranged – by nature? – to act like a catalyst, intervening between two more or less stable psychological states and causing them to change in a dramatic way. Seen from this point of view the Oedipal scenario is itself a kind of transitional object, playing the same role in secondary, social, identification that toys and other play objects do in primary identification. Whereas the first process involves identifying the self as a self, distinct from another, the second process makes important distinctions between various different kinds of others, and permits suitable allies to be recognised and potential enemies to be disarmed. In fact the process of identification is the true object rather than the social situations which give rise to it, for transitional objects depend on their safety. They are the safe solution to an urgent existential problem. Certainly, such objects, ideas, situations play a crucial role in the development of the creative imagination. They deserve a closer look.

Transitional objects lead us from the sphere of self-consciousness to that of other-consciousness. They function within a kind of mental space, 'potential space', and they depend on the proposition 'as if'. 'It is as if this nice smoothly rounded piece of wood, that lies in my toybox, in my special cupboard, were my mother. For me, when I'm playing with it, it is my mother.' Psychologically speaking, part of the child's own reality is transferred to, or projected onto the piece of wood, which is experienced as a separate object. Once its separateness is acknowledged, it can become the symbolic host of another separateness – namely that of the mother. This is a more frightening kind of difference; one that needs some kind of intermediary or buffer state. The wood serves two purposes, that of separating and that of joining, both of which are contained in the idea of *mediation*. Because it is experienced as neither one thing or the other, neither my own stick nor my mother's self, it is an invaluable and necessary go-between.

This is to endow an object, a piece of polished wood, with a personal identity, one like mine and mother's. It depends on the ability to *personify*, an obvious characteristic of the human awareness from this time onwards. It is always a way of expanding or widening human consciousness, although generally speaking it is regarded more favourably by poets than scientists. Artists have no difficulty in regarding their products as suitable or even privileged vehicles for their own personhood, and consequently that of those with whom they are in relationship. 'So long lives this, And this gives life to Thee' (Shakespeare, Sonnet XVIII). Poets may see not only their poems, but the natural or cultural setting in which they were composed, as reflecting the feelings that they express. What literary critics call 'the pathetic fallacy' ascribes sympathy to lakes, trees, forests and entire landscapes.

What the poet is doing is clear enough from the point of view of a dynamic psychology which recognises the importance of the self's ability to project its own characteristics of feeling and intention upon what is not itself, as a way of bolstering its own view of the situation and so protecting the autonomy of the individual ego. We use our imaginations to control our essential vulnerability. The mountains reflect my anguish: the universe understands and validates my state of mind. It validates *me*. This is something

I can do in order to make myself feel less lonely. Poets are only doing what everyone else does; giving a kind of spurious humanity to inanimate objects and non-human creatures so that they can claim them as allies in the war against vulnerability and uncontrolled impulse. From this point of view, 'works of the imagination' are considered to be psychological projections undertaken for the purpose of ego defence.

However, they are not experienced as such either by their authors or their audiences. To them, imagination is a gift rather than a product, and works of art messages from elsewhere, not extensions of the self. The products of my imagination have their own independent value; they are not merely another way of talking about my own concerns, a more striking way of putting my point of view. As Buber says, they are the place and time of an encounter with the other. Any psychology which takes account of the *experience* of art must be able to explain the phenomenon of otherness: what is not me, yet speaks to me, engaging my selfhood from elsewhere, not instrumentally but personally – certainly not reflexively or as a result of any initiative of my own except that of allowing myself to listen. We may approach the existential fact of inter-personal relationship from several directions, including those of humanistic psychotherapy and existentialist psychology, but the more direct route is through art.

This seems to us to raise the question of the independent reality of 'as if'. If imagination is not merely a convenient and rather self-indulgent expression of personal experience, an alternative way of talking about ourselves, we have to consider some of the judgements we habitually make about the nature of personal and social reality. Imagination is really another dimension of personal and social being, one which whenever I enter it releases me from my preoccupation with my own actions and intentions and sets me free to pursue the completeness I long for and do not find anywhere except in encounter with the otherness which establishes my own very separate personal identity. This is a doctrine of the imagination which allows it to perform a completely different role from that of an expression of the self – that of moving beyond itself to find a new way of being itself. The experience is not simply one of expanding the area or scope of the self, but of *leaving it behind*. Personifying the other requires being personified by otherness.

Personification involves bestowing independent life upon the object of the imagination. It means treating some of the contents of our imagination as if they were personal or even actual people; in other words imagining what other people think and feel. This seems to be required by an object relations view of human psychological development and it is certainly the experience of artists of all kinds. Social workers and professional carers call it empathy: 'Reactivating personal replicas of the emotion experienced by the other person' (Halmos, 1958, 24). Here the role of the imagination is to be a kind of creative matrix for relationships that are authentically personal. The culturally dominant view, however, values imagination as 'the source of blueprints for action in the world' – in other words, as having a wholly instrumental importance as the midwife of actual reality rather than any kind of reality in itself. Cartesian ideas about the primacy of understanding ensure that we continue to anchor every kind of human experience within an operational logic according to which selves act upon others, subjects upon objects, in fulfilment of a purpose or as part of a process.

One of the themes of this book will be the claim that in order to understand ourselves better we should pay more attention to our own experiences of works of art that have seized our imagination. Perhaps we ought to look again at the images that involve and entice us. Are they simply extensions of our own conscious egos, or do they participate in another, wider truthfulness? Are they in fact sacramental, participating in the reality to which they point? If our educated assumptions contradict our actual experiences, we should consider revising them.

The experience of theatre, the dramatic imagination focused and embodied, is a case in point. To restrict theatre to its role of passing on information or understanding from subject to object is gravely to misunderstand its nature and origins and neglect its crucial importance as a way of exploring relationship. Expressed and embodied, set free in the world, our imagination reflects its own origins whilst taking on a new identity. It is not simply another way in which we talk about ourselves, but a way in which something else talks to us; something we have forgotten and need to be reminded about: our timeless selves. If we concentrate hard on the life which is enacted before, around and among ourselves, we find ourselves entering a world of imagination which is our own and yet not our own – not ours in the language of possession and acquisition, or even analysis and interpretation, but in the sense of meanings that are immediate and unplanned. This world is both familiar and unfamiliar: as familiar as being alive, as unfamiliar as those special times when the world reveals itself to us as our natural intended home, not that which is explained to us by that which explains us. To 'seize and clutch and penetrate' is to destroy the kernel and be left holding the husk – in this case the play's own statement that it is 'only a play', and with this the feeling that you were foolish in wasting time in coming to see it. The only kind of violence involved in this is that demanded by any personal contact with another – what Derrida calls 'The irreducible violence of the relation to the other' which 'is at the same time non-violence, since it opens the relation to the other' (1978: 128, 9).

The life of literature and art, which comes to meet us when we approach it in the spirit of acceptance and enjoyment, delighting in its identity rather than our own, emerges from an experience primary to words. This remains true, however many words there may actually be in a play, a novel or a poem. It is not readily explicable unless we imagine that works of art exist in a world which we can visit because on one level of our existence we already live there and always have done. C.G. Jung claimed that this is in fact the case. We assume, he says, that our stories and images are our own conscious invention whereas the truth is very different. Jung regarded the imaginary figures that he encountered as though they were real people. 'The key is that 'as though', the metaphorical 'as if' reality, neither literally real or irreal/unreal...fully felt but wholly imaginary' (Hillman, 1983, 56). Jung uses 'as though' rather than 'as if', because he is concerned with experience rather than argument. The patterns of ideas which lie at the heart of folk and fairy tales, religious myths and legends throughout the world comprise a permanent heritage of essential understanding – understanding about being human. Just as each individual human life unfolds through a succession of events in time, so its trans-human metaphysical significance is enshrined in narrative. For us, narrative is a place of encounter; in dramatic stories we meet 'the ancient Gods that wish to penetrate our consciousness'. From time immemorial, our human impulse has been to locate truth in stories to which our own experience of a personal meaning which is delayed and so reflects back upon and includes an entire history within its scope, may somehow be homologized. James Hillman points to the tendency to see events in the form of human action, concentrating universal significance within the lives of heroes and heroines, kings and queens, orphans and witches, all of whom are archetypes of the collective unconscious, personifications of ultimate reality. To consider such stories as mere fiction is to misunderstand the way truth has always been communicated.

According to Hillman, writing in the Jungian tradition, we are conscious of the unexplained significance of works of art because of the activity of the human soul which is able to communicate with presences that can overcome the differentation that exists at the cognitive level of human experience. When we say 'as if', we reach out to the object of our imagination and discover that, in fact, it has the means to be in communion with us. We ourselves do not create it; it already exists and, in its soul, cries out for contact with us. We shall return to this in Chapter 4.

For Jung, the motifs of imagination and dream are metaphors not allegories. They tell their own stories and are 'not subject to interpretative translation without breaking their peculiar unity' (Hillman, 35). We find difficulty in taking them at face value and simply attending to their unique message because we have been indoctrinated into the strict subject–object interpretation of phenomena, and deny independent existence to anything which is not alive in the biological sense. In a metaphor two realities, one concrete, the other spiritual, join forces and speak in a new voice. So far as we are concerned, however, whether we are idealists or empiricists, we are the only life-givers. The world of actual experience is rather different, however. If we are willing to abandon our conclusions and trust our senses we may rediscover the world as it was before we disenchanted it – the world we live in and which lives in us, that opens itself up to us as beings and not simply minds or nervous systems. 'Farewell, rewards and Fairies,' says the Stuart poet Richard Corbet, bemoaning a doctrinaire Puritanism that was busy stamping out the ancient 'superstitions' that enlivened country life. 'Yet who of late for cleanliness Finds sixpence in her shoe?' Psychologically speaking, the world of imagination, of fairy rewards and angelic visitors, is not to be divorced from that of demonstrable reality. In scientifically unsophisticated cultures, as in childhood, the two are acknowledged to be interdependent. Imagination is not simply a commentary upon public events but an important and necessary way in which we come to terms with life. It is not public but it is certainly shared, as even the shallowest study of folk traditions and religious systems reveals. Because it refers to a reality greater than our individual awareness, we are its creatures as well as its shapers, and its inhabitants address us before we speak to them, not to dominate or control, but always in one way or another to influence us.

The landscape Corbet loved, and that he commemorates in his poem, is the one described three centuries later by Maurice Merleau-Ponty (1962) who proclaims it as man's true home, the reality of our actual experience of the world – that it is in relation to us, as we are to it. The world responds to us as if it has a life of its own. For Merleau-Ponty, perception is the awareness not of ideas or objects, but of the actual principle of relationship. He speaks of 'the natural and ante-predicative unity of the world and our life'. We do not make the world, nor are we made by it; our life is always in mutuality with it. This has startling effects, experiences that are inexplicable in the language of mind alone. It is our body that responds primarily to the things we live among (including, of course, the bodies of other people); we know about human reality with our body which finds its way in the world, anchoring our minds to the kinds of sensory awareness that intellectuals despise, providing them with experience of belonging in the tangible, kinetic, sensory world that thinking could not otherwise provide for us. It is the world, says Merleau-Ponty, that makes us real. It is our home, our setting. What we inherit psychologically is recognisable in actual objects, animals and people. They do not exist because of our ability to draw conclusions about them, any more than we exist because the forces of nature have given us birth. For us, existence is belonging together and complementing each other, exposing our own nature and abilities by using the other's language. No account may be given of a human being, says Merleau-Ponty, that is independent of his or her relations with the world. The world reaches out to give us reality and receive our meanings – a statement that is equally true when we put it the other way round.

The way that we understand things like this, things that belong to our identity as human beings, embodied spirits, is by using our imaginations, which it seems do not entirely belong to us. No other faculty will do. Pirandello describes how the reality of the people he describes in his play *Six Characters in Search of an Author* consists in their having taken personal life in his own imagination. This life is genuinely their own, even when it is expressed in the flesh and blood of the people actually performing the play. In other words, his imagination has given birth to something entirely new. Who 'fathered' these people? *That* is beyond his imagination...

We find ourselves saying with Hamlet, that 'There are more things in heaven and earth than are dreamed of in your philosophy' (1.v). Nowadays this would seem to be true of most of our philosophy. Archetypal psychology sees the world in a more inclusive way and values imagination more highly than most reductionist approaches. In the shared world of the imagination, 'as if' achieves epistemological value as a way of approaching human truth. The imaginative personification of archetypal images is encounter rather than escape, not simply a form of self-expression but the consummation of a relationship with the source of truths that may be ultimate and salutary. The meaning of life is not concealed from us, but simply presented in the form of the metaphor.

CHAPTER 2

Metaphor

The Artistic Use of As If

Metaphor provides us with a way of expressing the otherwise inexpressible. In a metaphor about jewels, Christopher Marlowe talks of 'Infinite riches within a little room' (*The Jew of Malta* 1.1.36). He might just as well have been describing metaphor itself. In metaphor 'as if' takes on the ability to point in two ways at once, carrying us along with it by using things we know as a way of directing us towards what we cannot grasp – or cannot grasp yet. Literally speaking, of course, our brain cannot grasp anything. Unless of course we use 'grasp' in a special way. Unless we use it metaphorically. A metaphor is a carrying from one place to another.

'Meta' itself means 'with'; in a metaphor, a thing, a person. an idea, a word, carries something else along with it, usually something else that cannot be grasped by itself without its 'carrying word': its metaphor. Metaphor does not stand instead of something else but carries something else along with it. A mountain of work is both a huge amount of things to be done, and a mountain – or at least the idea of a mountain. It is neither the one nor the other because it is both. Metaphors are links, not substitutes. To use Shakespeare's phrase they can be 'ciphers to a great accompt', or they can simply be used to point to things that are in some way similar and consequently, to that extent, shareable. 'Great accompts' which lie outside our ability to grasp, can be imagined; and if they can be imagined they can be metaphorically shared.

On the other hand, their manner of sharing will always be oblique rather than straightforward. They are a way round the communication barrier rather than a way through. In a sense, they go straight to the *meaning* instead of being deflected by things that stand in its way. The things that stand in the way are held aside so that encounter can take place: 'The creative spark of the metaphor does not spring from the presentation of live signifiers equally actualized. It flashes between two signifiers, one of which has taken place of another in the signifying chain, the occulted signifier remaining present through its connection with the rest of the chain' (Lacan, 1977). In other words a connection which would otherwise have been dominant and intrusive has been distanced by one which is less specific but still *extremely relevant*. In George Steiner's phrase, it demands 'not obeisance but a live echo' (1969, 101).

With regard to the individual brain's relationship to the entire universe, and to itself, of course, there is no way in which it can make contact with what is not itself without using intermediaries. It uses thoughts, feelings, intuitions. It uses words and linguistic codes. It uses social and personal systems. It expands its ways of affecting its environment, whatever is not itself, by developing itself and consequently the range of behaviour which is at its disposal. A cognitive psychologist has said that 'All biological forms and all human conceptual systems are transformations of metaphenomena from the realm of possible, to actual existence' (Antaki and Lewis, 1986, 98). By 'metaphenomena' Lewis means 'whatever is implied but still not realised'. Metaphors are the first things we make and the first things with which we make anything else. They are our initial problems, our primary plans and our first real actions. We make them with our minds, which at this stage are all we have to make them with.

We are used to regarding metaphor as a literary technique, a way in which poets give extra dimensions of meaning and experience to whatever it may be that they are describing, including things that are not there within their recognition of what is present. Metaphor, however, precedes our ability to use words, never mind write them down as literature. It originates in right brain activity, the hemisphere which apprehends meaning without recourse to words, and by which we know intuitively, discovering by creating rather than recording. It is a function of our creative selves; logic, reasoning, linguistic codes, the works of the left brain may use it but they certainly never invented it. It is questionable whether they invent anything. The fact that all words refer to things apart from themselves makes literary metaphor less immediate than the left brain's use of objects, places, persons or things in the world which allows them to be themselves without describing them, before using them to point beyond themselves. A pile of books can be seen as 'a mountain of work' without having to spell the picture out in any way.

We may go further than this, however. 'Metaphor...is a human act of feeling towards and giving shape and understandability to that which is sensed but not yet known in this particular form' (Mair, 1989, 72,3). Writing from the stand-point of clinical psychology, Mair speaks of the importance of 'encouraging people to pretend, *to act as if*... With access to metaphor and play, and permission to value what may otherwise be crushed into a banal rejection of meaning, a person can begin to find a voice to give shape and colour, pattern and coherence to what they feel but never before have been able to say.' Thus, metaphor has a psychoformative function which is frequently ignored; for human culture is not a literal description of or prescription for life, but a closely interwoven web of inter-related meanings which we as individuals can either use or be used by in our search for personal truth. Human understanding is not simply ingested and stored for future use but is a way in which we 'take on, put on, try on, lay over ourselves, the creative undertakings of others' (Mair, 1989, 203). Human freedom subsists in the ability of individuals to choose these metaphors which will either liberate or constrict them. Once the metaphorical nature of something is recognised, it can be either chosen or rejected; because metaphor is not an imposed 'official' interpretation of reality, but the expression of an insight that is personal and individual – in Mair's phrase 'a rule-breaking procedure'.

The theatrical symbol preserves its identity as recognisable metaphor, avoiding that reduction to the literal which deadens and misleads. It does this by using techniques which are, at their purest and most truly theatrical, non-verbal. The actions and gestures of the actor are the most potent and eloquent statement available to the dramatist; the living metaphors which allow theatrical knowing. They have a directness and an absence of ambiguity denied to any purely verbal communication, an unparalleled immediacy which resists and eludes rubricisation and rationalisation. In the dramatic experience 'the human gesture is its own ultimate extension, and can be apprehended immediately by the human participant, without the interposition of thought or artifact' (Grossvogel, 1962, 180).

Our metaphor is ourselves, for 'No intellectual process is either as immediate or as assertive as the flesh' (Grossvogel, 1962, 183). The total theatrical event is 'flesh-creating'. Aristotle's conception of the existential power of theatre as 'concrete philosophy' asserts as much. Here, language breaks the bond of literature, and, as in life, becomes an 'extension of human gesture'. It is now no longer used to tame experience, but to expand it in a living way which involves a direct encounter between people. An intellectualist theatre, aiming at making its points by an appeal to cognition alone, is unrealisable, for the theatrical symbol is a metaphor for what is otherwise inexpressible, rather than being one of a number of alternative convenient or illuminating ways of getting meaning across – as in spoken description, mathematical formulae, pictorial illustration and so on. Metaphor reveals meaning; dramatic metaphor creates a place for meaning to happen in. The clearer the dramatic structure, the more powerful the metaphor.

In his 'space–time theory' of theatrical experience Wilson Knight attempted to explain the peculiar impact of the dramatic event by drawing attention to the dimension of emotional depth provided by the *form* of theatre, which imposes limits according to a set sequence of events within a set time. Knight maintained that this closed time sequence has the effect of *turning the emotional significance in upon itself*, or of crystallising it and formalising it to become a new, metaphorical 'third dimension':

> the third space dimension of solidity and realism corresponds to the extra dimension of psychic reality unveiled or created by poetry – and this is dependent upon the form of the play, its set limits and conventions… Conventionally limited the stage becomes a magic area, where every action and position is deeply significant. Neither the spatial nor the temporal gets at the play's essential quality which exists in mental space-time. By using and welcoming the stage convention, freely and simply, you can do things impossible otherwise – all is done by positive visual suggestion in terms of the convention. (Knight, 1936, 71)

Thus the play's identity as a *conventional use of time and space* has to be preserved in order to establish its metaphorical force. By their manner of staging and acting, plays must proclaim their nature as narrative metaphor.

On the other hand, if it is used in a way that is antipathetic to the full humanness of actor and spectator, metaphor may become the enemy of theatrical truth. Such plays as those of Jean Genet, in which the use of symbolism is so potent that the relationship of actor and spectator is heightened to become 'the relationship of phantasts to sacred object' (Grossvogel, 1962, 139) represent the apotheosis of theatre *as a technique*. All drama represents a balance between truth or actuality and illusion, manipulated to arrive at an illusion which is truth, the truth of relationship and meeting. In this kind of theatre the force of wish fulfilment on the spectator's part strengthens the inevitable and necessary illusion of character and role, so that the otherness of the actor, his factual, personal being is drained of its own authentic life, and becomes 'the image of a precious illusion,' possessing a fraudulent life – the life of the spectator's private phantasy. The actor no longer stands between the truth of the spectator and the illusion of the role, giving the latter the blessing of his own truth; he is reduced by the author to a fellow-worshipper with the spectator at the shrine of the victorious libido, where he shares his experiences with the spectator, indulging his schizoid craving for a reality which cannot be his except in mime, in illusion. Thus Genet aims at a theatre of significances and symbols *per se*, in which the mind of the spectator is led backwards and inwards through a maze of roles and appearances in order to enjoy a world of make-believe, for its own sake, a world which is both potent and satisfactory.

'Genet's characters,' says Grossvogel, 'must be apprehended as significances, objects of fascination, not as people' (1962, XVII). We may not ignore the fact that the living part of the stage is the human reality of the actors. But the life of the theatre is not lessened or weakened by its 'persona' of artistic form. In all art we have a concrete and living embodiment of the universal, particularized in sense; in the drama, the content to which form is married in the living reality of human beings. Man, himself a unity of matter and spirit, participates in the incarnationality of art, and this most vital fact of his nature – his own incarnationality – is most clearly revealed there. If theatre is to remain true to itself as the irreducible iconography of human existence, symbolic communication may not be used impersonally to distort and manipulate relationship. Genet's symbols are emphatically *not* persons, but ideas – they do not depend for their hypnotic power upon the common flesh of humanity, which separates and allows relation, but on the dangerous inclusionism of shared phantasy.

The factual, concrete, psychosomatic presence of the actor constitutes a check upon the free phantasy of the imagined character he plays, but it is by no means a final check. If the theatre gives up the human element in its enticement of man, it is faced with the choice between symbolic manipulation – as in Genet's plays – and an openness or transparency of image which leaves the spectator as much as possible to his own devices – that is, to what he himself brings. It is certainly possible for a man to meet himself in the phantasy world of an auto-theatrical experience; but it is only when the symbol upon the stage has its own intransigent and uncompromising human reality, a reality which is completely personal and completely other, that theatre may be truly life-expanding and therapeutic. Thus, either by neglect of metaphorical potential, as in over-naturalistic theatre, or by its abuse, as in the 'total' symbolism of Genet, theatre may forfeit its possibilities as a means of producing 'involvement-through-otherness' and consequently of inspiring valid and healing relationships. The forces of theatre may be misused, either in the direction of a wasted opportunity, as in the dulling of imaginative involvement by a photographic realism, or in that of depriving the spectator of action and reality by involving him all too effectively in a world existing *at his expense*, a world of crippling illusion which instead of giving him life, takes life from him.

In our generation of Western civilization, as in others before ours going back at least to the Renaissance, metaphor is distrusted as a way of communicating things that are reliable and 'true' (Jennings, 1990, 15). We rate science and technology higher than art and religion. The attitudes of those who study human responses to the world range from dismissing metaphor as a 'mentalistic' illusion, something produced by human behaviour but in no way responsible for bringing it about, to regarding it as a significant factor in human communication, an inherent and pervasive factor in human understanding. Marianne Gassel, in her exploration of the use of metaphor as an educational tool, argues that while learning based on intellectual and scientific language risks the loss of flexibility, the use of metaphor which communicates on many levels is 'un bon véhicule pour les savoirs, les savoir-faire et les savoir-être' (1994, 15). In other words, metaphor enables us to learn not just how to do, but also how to be. 'Almost all therapy', says John Flowers 'can be viewed as a simulation of the client's real life' (1975, 59). Many therapists regard the part of their lives that their clients share with them as a kind of metaphor. The therapeutic relationship is concentrated on a small portion of interpersonal experience, from which conclusions will be drawn about all the rest; whatever the client says or does now, however he or she reacts to the situation or set of circumstances, will be both itself and something else, a reaction at once specific and general. In other words this sample of behaviour acts as a metaphor for behaviour as a whole, so far as this person is concerned. We are talking here, of course, about therapies of the kind in which a professional therapist attempts to 'understand' his or her client. In other kinds of therapy the therapist may encourage the client to see present behaviour as a metaphor of possible behaviour that could be adopted, or as itself possessing a metaphorical identity which gives it value and meaning. In all these cases 'as if' is given artistic form in the shape of a bridging presence, able to include idea and actuality within the same image. In other words, a metaphor.

Metaphor, then, is a particular kind of symbol, one that 'participates in that to which it points'. Metaphors are not symbols in a mathematical sense; in other words, they are not simply signs for something else, but always refer to two things, two worlds, one of which is to be contacted according to the way in which it stands towards the other. Because it can be used to infer something of infinitely wider scope than something we know about – and is only understood at all in its *contrast* with what we know about – this is usually associated with a religious or sacramental use of symbol. However, metaphoric symbolism is available for coming to terms with other kinds of unthinkable truths. In particular it comes to our aid in situations of mental and emotional agony – terror, fear, grief, despair.

Metaphor has a Janus quality, so that it looks two ways at once, facing in two directions. The things it signifies pivot on the signifier. This becomes obvious when we compare literary and dramatic metaphors. Literary metaphor is convergent, facing inwards upon itself in order to clarify the meaning of what is being said. If, instead of talking about 'a lot of work' or 'a huge amount of work' we say 'a mountain of work', we are concentrating attention on the impression of size that we want to convey to the listener or reader. It is a specific impression that we want to give, not a specific size. Metaphor is never literal. We want to transmit a very definite idea about an overpowering amount of work, too much work, and that is how the image is received by the reader or listener, who knows precisely what we mean. Dramatic metaphor, the metaphors used in dramatherapy, on the other hand, are intended to widen horizons rather than focus understanding. The focussing is brought about by the concentration of imagination upon which drama depends. Within this setting, however, objects and people are themselves and more than themselves – they acquire a resonance which leads the imagination far beyond the given circumstances of the drama's presentation, even of the drama itself. The aim of the metaphor is possibility and freedom, the abandoning of ordinary constraints on the imagination. Instead of being reminded of what we knew and have experienced, we are carried away into what we *could* know, *what could be our experience*... The chair could be a mountain, the empty floor an ocean – but it would be a mountain and an ocean we had certainly never climbed or crossed before, one which had never existed anywhere except in our imagination...

To put it like this is to distort the truth somewhat. It is not as clear cut as this by any means. Both kinds of metaphor point both ways, as symbolism always does. Descriptive literary metaphors lead us outwards to a newer, richer understanding of what life may hold; evocative dramatic metaphor reflects back on our actual experience, the things, situations and people that set our imaginations going. Mary Douglas, writing about the use of ritual in so-called 'primitive' societies, speaks of 'the pivoting of symbolism' (1973). Corporate symbols are acted metaphors, the non verbal presentation of the primal act of imagination which consists of *the awareness of what is not immediate within immediacy itself*, not simply as an argument, the primary logical deduction, or the even more primitive recognition that for something to be itself there must be at least one other thing for it to be distinguished from or seen over against – but as a *presence*. As something here and now, the thing that allows it to be itself.

If imagination is the source of drama, then metaphor is the point at which it begins to work in a recognisably dramatic way. In metaphor we have the origin of a world which is here and not here, people who are me and not me, a time which is now and hereafter or long ago. In metaphor we have the possibility of conflicting forces or presences which are held in tension without being confused or synthesised into something else – in other words we have a scenario that is lifelike, characterised by constrictions and possibilities, limited joys and pain that may be survived, defeats and victories, problems and solutions. The double identity of metaphor allows us to use it as a means of healing. Because they both refer to what is safe and familiar, and yet remind us of things that lie outside what we know and have learned how to manage, things that terrify and dismay us, metaphors disarm our worst fears and bring us into the presence of what we dread so much, yet must somehow acknowledge. However, before we say it *only* happens there, we ought to reflect that imagination is the site of our worst fears and most crippling inhibitions.

In fact there is much more involved in this than the presence of a comforting fantasy of safety and satisfaction which has the ability to distract us from ideas of danger or pain. Metaphor originates in imagination but it has power to move us out of our preoccupation with thinking and feeling 'in' ourselves, into a world of actual encounter with what lies beyond us, the relationships with people and things that make us people by making us real. If trauma or despair turns us in on ourselves, the power inherent in symbolism directs us to the source of our defeat, the thing we cannot contemplate, much less come to terms with. Some years ago, writing about the shock and disruption of bereavement, I said that 'symbolism is a kind of expanded thought capable of bearing an emotional load that would otherwise remain inexpressible precisely because it is unthinkable. The symbol enables us to come to terms on an intuitive level with facts whose literal meaning we cannot yet deal with. Its use is to convey a particular kind of message, one which cannot be encoded in any other way because its significance is too powerful for words' (Grainger, 1988, 30).

I backed up what I had said by drawing attention to what Carl Jung says about symbolism's power to point beyond the individual to the other, including within its reference the known, the unknown and the unknowable. The symbols described by Jung exert their healing power at the pre-verbal level of our unconscious awareness. They are the unspoken metaphors of the meaning of reality which he calls archetypes. As we shall see later on, archetypal awareness comes to the mind's surface when the urge for healing is at its most powerful. At these times, our natural ability to 'see' things that happen to us as bearers of a message about the meaning and value of our life as a whole – what we might call our metaphorical sense – provides our unconscious symbolism with an opportunity for conscious expression.

For example, metaphor helps bereaved people make contact with the emotional sense of what has happened to them, so that they can begin the real business of grieving. What Freud calls 'griefwork' can only take place when we have a real apprehension of what has happened to us – what it is that we need to work on. Real futures cannot be built on un-realised presents; which is why we often find ourselves having to work so hard to catch up with a position in chronological time that we have not yet reached emotion-ally. An example of the use of metaphor in grief-therapy is the following story:

> Mrs King had spent almost 20 years nursing her brain-damaged son, whose father had abandoned her as soon as he discovered that she was pregnant. She had given up hope of ever getting married, and regarded her single parent status as a kind of punishment for having had an illegitimate child – particularly one who was, in her words, 'born to suffer'. In her mid-forties, however, she met the man who became her husband, and fell in love. She felt that she had at last found someone who really understood and accepted her. He divorced his wife and married Mrs King, who was overcome with joy and gratitude for the way her life had changed. At last she knew what it was like to be really happy. The couple went away on honeymoon to a cottage by the sea. At this point, tragedy struck – Mr King had a heart attack and was rushed to hospital where he died almost immediately. Mrs King went back alone to the cottage and got onto the bed that they had shared. Part of the ceiling in the room in which she was lying began to cave in… For months and even years afterwards she could only think about what had happened in terms of the collapsed ceiling:

MRS KING: I was just lying in bed. I couldn't take anything in you know, I didn't know what had happened at all. And then it just happened.

COUNSELLOR: What happened, Mrs King? Can you tell me?

MRS KING: It was the roof. It just fell in. Part of the ceiling of the room began to fall in. I had to move, I couldn't stay there. The roof fell in and I had to move house…

The counsellor records that 'During the course of over thirty weekly interviews the incident was mentioned three times. On two occasions Mrs King went on to express resentment against her family for their attitude to her husband and to criticise God for his unfair treatment of herself.' He goes on to note that 'Later on in her bereavement Mrs King started to get to work decorating her house. She did not manage to get very far with this before she was forced to give up by the impact of her emotions.' Eventually, however, much later in the course of the interviews, the memory of this attempt to 'get her house in order', and the anger and frustration it had caused her, led Mrs King to discover the real force of her grief at the loss of her husband. The counsellor comments to the effect that 'An event or an idea which is so symbolic of the collapse into chaos often serves to express an understanding which cannot yet be faced but must somehow be acknowledged' (Grainger, 1979, 205).

Bereavement counselling is, of course, only one area in which metaphors carry out this enabling task. There are some experiences which are so psychologically disruptive that any non-metaphorical description seems woefully inadequate and 'clinical'. Writing about having worked with sufferers from Post Traumatic Stress Disorder, a condition caused by events which need not necessarily involve an actual death, but are nevertheless felt to be 'world shattering', Linda Winn says

> If I am offered a metaphor during debriefing, I may stay with it for a while. For example, one person spoke of feeling as if he was walking through thick treacle, with more weight being added to his boots all the time and the light being blocked out. I later referred to the treacle and weight and he responded that he was having difficulty getting the treacle off and the weight was still quite heavy, but he was no longer sinking, and could see some light. (1994, 41)

In these examples, taken from ordinary human situations, we can see that metaphor is itself a kind of drama. Time and again, it is a way of resolving conflict; in this case that which exists between perception and denial, the defensive reaction which exists to protect the sensitive balance of feelings and thoughts which is our emotional and cognitive way of dealing with life, our psychological homoeostasis, and the need to take account of what has happened in a realistic way in order to survive – the innate *courage to be*, even in the face of defeat. The resolution of conflict does not always have to be dramatic, of course; but the painful victory of life over death which takes place actually within the metaphor itself, as defeat slowly becomes challenge, is precisely the kind of idea which drama takes hold of and on which it builds. Metaphor is dramatic in that it allows a psychological process to take on a visual (aural, tactile, kinetic) identity, something not itself yet communicating truth about itself – embodying its reality in the shape, weight and texture of the concrete world. In this primary bridging of idea and object which expresses both the initial opposition and the gradual movement towards resolution and a new reality we have the origin of art in general and drama in particular. Every metaphor is a symbolic arena, a world of interaction, a stage for drama.

Metaphor 'helps a patient come as close to his true feelings as he dares' (Cox and Theilgaard, 1987, 9). The urge to disclose the hidden source of their pain can be very strong in disturbed patients. Cox and Theilgaard describe the use of literary metaphor in a way that is both divergent and convergent. 'exploratory and supportive'. What they call the Aeolian Mode of psychotherapy uses poetry (*poiesis*) to 'reach out to the mind's deeps without disturbing the surface', so that psychological change may take place while leaving the patient's carefully constructed defences unbreached. Verbal communication 'affords safety, in that gratification experience does not slide towards engulfment. Neither does "affectionate distancing" become "malignant abandonment" (1987, 196). As we shall see, this kind of balance corresponds to the conditions necessary for the achievement of catharsis. The poetic image may evoke echoes within the patient able to short-circuit channels of communication that have become blocked by the patient's need to protect him or herself from pain. This is because the poetry actually posesses a specificity that literal discourse lacks; we find in it 'an exact sense of fit and detached engagement' because of, not in spite of 'its conscious openness and potential for particularity' (1987, 63). The openness of the poetic mode encourages the patient 'to tell his story so that disclosure can lead to a change in the way he sees himself and his world.' ...Poetic metaphor 'carries a particular affective loading' which 'resonates with that within the patient which is called into existence' (1987, 5, 23). This only happens, however, 'at the point of urgency'. It is as if our need for disclosure takes the opportunity provided by the openness and generality of the poetic metaphor to allow it to speak for us in a very particular and personal way. 'The heavily defended psychopath and the psychotic patient seem to respond because their perception of the inner and outer world is made more flexible and encouraging through the use of image and the mutative metaphor' (1987, 124). Again, the metaphor both distances us from our pain and lets us communicate with it. Transcendent meaning eludes our defensiveness by including it.

Metaphor, of course, is not just a tool for illuminating the client's awareness; it acts equally on that of the therapist. Cox and Theilgaard eloquently demonstrate how metaphor (and here they refer primarily to metaphor derived from the works of Shakespeare) provides a rich source of prompting for the therapist when the therapeutic narrative breaks down: '...Shakespeare prompts the therapist when his fine-tuning can detect the signal. And the therapist can be regarded as the patient's prompter, who intervenes when language begins to fail...Shakespeare then serves as the prompter's prompter' (1994, 95). The prompting, however, is not just a matter of enabling the client to find words to express meaning; it also focuses on the cadences and rhythms of speech, the whole complex and multi-layered business of communication. Cox and Theilgaard show us how Shakespeare's words can pierce the confusion and throw into relief the things that we could not see before, or did not see in the same way; in their words '...one of the reasons why Shakespeare is so powerful a prompter to the creativity of the therapist is because he frequently adopts unexpected alignments of reality and fantasy in order to make a point' (1994, 56).

As they demonstrate, a profound understanding of the plays, characters, language and imagery of Shakespeare illuminates our awareness of humanity; of human acts, thoughts and feelings, and provides us with the common creative ground where we can allow ourselves to encounter perhaps the most disturbing and destructive acts, thoughts and feelings of all. It is important to stress their point that they do not advocate using Shakespeare as a source of '*a priori* ready-made-answers – a 'collection of good quotations'...' to be dipped into when the therapist is at a loss for words. On the contrary, they show us how prompting arises out of an awareness of the multiple associations that are generated from the client, his background and his history, and that the process of prompting is a synthesis which cannot be based on 'rational thinking' alone: 'In order to do justice to the many-layered meaningfulness, the therapist, the patient and the actor have to rely on their unconscious. And Shakespeare's poetry takes us to the depth' (Cox and Theilgaard, 1994, 216). Indeed, it is Shakespeare's own precision, that contained accuracy that Alexander Pope described as 'What oft was thought but ne'er so well expressed' that provides us with a sharp instrument to enhance our clinical precision.

Shakespeare, perhaps more than any other writer, has portrayed humankind in such a rich and vibrant way that his work has penetrated our culture and embedded itself firmly in the unconscious. His metaphors could be called 'great' metaphors in that they have achieved sufficient universality and psychological depth to become archetypal. He does not, of course have the monopoly here, but perhaps his metaphors have particular significance for us, as his personages and stories are comparatively close to us historically; far closer than those characters who populate the myths, legends and religious texts that are the prime sources of archetypes. But let us not forget the 'small' metaphors, the symbolism of the familiar and the everyday. These metaphors arise out of what is around us, what is immediately available to us, but yet have the capacity to point towards that which lies hidden. It is when they become enacted that they attain their full power. The use of metaphor that Cox and Theilgaard write about is literary metaphor, albeit from a theatrical background and informed by dramatic process. Their therapeutic approach is based in a traditional psychotherapy whose healing element is poesis. When poetry takes on human flesh in performance, once the metaphor becomes an acted metaphor, it has an immediacy of human contact that is unique; the laminations of literature that are held rigid upon the page are transformed into a living matrix which allows movement within itself – where unfamiliar things rise to the surface and the familiar may become submerged... Where new horizons become possible.

If we look back to the beginning of this book, we may trace a definite progression of ideas which corresponds to the development of awareness, from the undifferentiated perception of the infant's original image making to the first movements according to which other people are distinguished from the self, and imagination comes into existence as a state of affairs in which things happen as if they were happening to the self; to the ability to believe that things and people can signify a reality other than our own; finally to the power to create a world in which people and things are at one and the same time different from and the same as oneself and also different from and yet the same as themselves. In this way we learn first to imagine, then to believe in a state of affairs apart from the immediate one, and then to create a setting for it. The ability to find comfort in mental pictures, images, goes back a long way, perhaps to the very beginning; and the power to let the known and the unknown fight it out within the confines of a single image may be something we have possessed from our very early childhood. It certainly fulfils an essential function in our psychological economy, for it filters the unknown through the known, the unacceptable through the comfortingly familiar. In psychotherapy, it can be a way of allowing private universes to adjust to worlds that are shared with others. A single metaphor may encapsulate a mind at war with itself.

How does this kind of intrapsychic use of metaphor relate to story, theatre and religious ritual, all of them interpsychic phenomena? As individuals, we use metaphor as a technique for coping with things that we cannot allow ourselves to know in the ordinary, straightforward way in which we usually perceive the world about us. It is a way of containing and distancing perception in order to come to terms with whatever it is that temporarily defeats us. In much the same way we tell one another stories which contain the familiar and the strange, the comforting and the terrifying, the trivial and the cataclysmic within a single narrative structure which, because it is recognised as a work of conscious art, in this case a story *about* life, protects us from all that we would be forced to think and feel if these things were happening not to the people in the story, but to us. It is the narrative convention that distances and contains. In reference to the act of storytelling and of listening, Marianne Gassel describes the experience as 'une merveilleuse aventure au cours de laquelle conteur et auditeur(s) vibrent ensemble en une profonde communion' (1994, 15). This comes into force as soon as the narrator takes up his book and opens it, or assumes his or her customary storytelling attitude, the way she or he always sits or stands when about to start telling a story, the special tone of voice which always signifies story-telling, whether or not we actually hear the words *once upon a time...*

In whatever guise the two presences appear, genuine stories are always about life and death. In other words, they are about the things which in our own lives we are used to employing metaphors to deal with. The problem to be solved is in the story itself, which is always about a conflict, the basic opposition between what can or cannot be endured – the same story expressed by the metaphor's single image. In the story this metaphor is extended and elaborated, using the skill needed to put together a story out of an *ad hoc* collection of structural elements, adjusting motive and character, time and place, even the order in which events are presented, in order to make the problem and its resolution as striking as possible.

In itself, then, the story possesses the elements of metaphor, bringing the unliveable into contact with what is already being lived. The problem it enshrines is made more approachable by the skill which goes into presenting it as a story – something carefully put together and skilfully narrated – and also, of course, by the human presence of the story-teller. All these things distance the listeners from the terrors that the story records. Here we have a second level of metaphor, centred upon the distance between the story and its listeners, brought about by the action of story-telling itself, the presentation of the story as a story. When this is redistributed among actors while retaining its identity as a presentation, we have theatre, a kind of acted story telling.

This second level of narrative metaphor, centred upon the actual distance between the fictional world of the story or the play, and the real world of an audience aware of the nature of the proceedings, is the one at which the true theatre of metaphor functions. As theatre, it communicates kinaesthetically, using right brain awareness to by-pass the left brain preoccupation with the literal. Semmes (1968) contrasts the 'focal' representation of phenomena carried out by the left hemisphere of the brain with right brain function which, he says, 'permits an integration of dissimilar units'. Thus associations which are left unmade by the left brain because of the painful dissonance that would ensue, may perhaps be carried out kinaesthetically in the right hemisphere. Theatre and drama contact the right brain directly, before engaging in argument with the left one! At this level of distance from the world of the story, the spectator is able both to imagine him or herself *into* that world and to imagine *beyond* it; to identify the happenings in the story as at least potentially similar to her or his own situation and to regard this dramatic enactment as a metaphor not just for their own life but life in general, seen from a position in which we are privileged to regard it as a whole. The drama becomes a parable, something 'thrown alongside' life, in which the problems of the people in the play are recognised as the problem of life itself – the most profound problem of all. This is achieved, not by analysis of the difficulty set before us, but by entering into it ourselves – 'The paradox of gaining entry (to life) from a starting point deep within,' so that our well defended thresholds of thought and feeling are 'crossed from inside, rather than outside' (Cox and Theilgaard, 1987; 162).

This is the drama of *Oedipus Rex, King Lear,* and *Waiting for Godot,* all of which and countless others are acted parables. It depends on many things, the most important of which, perhaps, is the distance provided by their metaphoric identity. In theatre this is lived out by real people, not simply ideas, or imaginary personages. Theatre presents us with a special kind of metaphor. As Bruce Wilshire (1982) says 'Characters enacted on stage are not verbal but physionomic metaphors: we see and feel them to be like ourselves'. He goes on to claim that 'the whole point of art is to put us in touch with things that are too far off or too close.' – or too overwhelming – 'for us to see in our off-stage life.' His image of theatre holding up a mirror to human life is compelling, for metaphor itself is a mirror – but it is not a mirror that is held directly up to us, face on. It is a mirror held at an oblique angle that enables us to see what we could not see otherwise. Theatre lets us look into this mirror almost accidentally; we do not necessarily go to the theatre with the precise intention of looking at ourselves. It is within therapy that we find the courage to gaze into the back-view mirror held up to us by the therapist or the group. Even then, we find ourselves peering into the mirror that we believe is capturing another's reflection, only to be startled by our own – an unlooked-for image that is unmodified by self-consciousness.

It is this kind of dramatic metaphor that dramatherapists use and dramatherapy explores. It does not depend on words, which may 'prevent, obscure and edit experience' (Cox and Theilgaard, 1987; 188). A basic dramatherapeutic process involves the creation of acted metaphor. The scope of such an approach is as wide as imagination itself. Because it is acted and not simply thought about, private metaphor becomes a kind of public reality. Fantasy becomes communication by means of the dramatic symbol. This is the heart of the method – if this individual approach can be called 'methodical'. At the same time, the imagery of dramatherapy is candid about its identity as symbolism, and lays no claim to being the reality it points to and imaginatively shares in. It is always drama: belief is optional, participation by invitation only. Like ritual, dramatherapy proclaims its own limitations: it is only a play. It is essentially metaphoric, embodying a view of life that does not approach meaning head-on, to tame and reduce it, but lives imaginatively and creatively *with* meanings until human truth is ready to emerge.

CHAPTER 3

Suspending Disbelief

With regard to theatre, 'as if' signifies belief in the lifelike quality of what is taking place on stage. Coleridge (1817, Ch14) puts it in another way, reminding us that theatre functions according to the principle of 'the willing suspension of disbelief'. What he is saying is that we should be willing for the time being to ignore the guidelines provided by our assumptions about the difference between imagination and reality, and allow ourselves to believe, for the course of the play, that the life presented to us within its action is continuous with our own, so that we are not simply interested, but involved and concerned. We must be prepared to believe that these could be events in our own life, otherwise we shall not enjoy theatre as we are meant to do. We should be willing to believe in another, less immediate reality than ours, communicated to us by our imaginative involvement in the happenings on-stage.

This, according to Coleridge (1817), is the *sine qua non* of theatre-going.[1] Otherwise we might just as well stay at home. The theatre he was asking us to believe in – assuming we would believe in – is not easy to mistake for anything else. Its limitations as an imitation of life outside the theatre building were plain to see in cases where disbelief remained unsuspended. Coleridge was writing in the early part of the nineteenth century, before the advent of naturalism. His was no 'fourth wall' theatre; the actors he went to see and hear had not been trained in the New York 'Actors' Studio'. The realism of the world that they created was that of basic theatricality, expecting and gaining our willingness to co-operate in suspending our disbelief because it was the essence of the whole theatrical enterprise.

It certainly seems to be the case that this 'basic theatricality' exerts an influence upon imagination that naturalism often fails to do. Theatre puts us

---

1   'That willing suspension of disbelief for the moment that constitutes poetic faith.'

in a position where we have to make a definite decision: do we suspend disbelief or not? The decision is crucial, for empathy with the people in the play must be freely given, or it will not be empathy at all. Unless our imagination is freely engaged there is no theatre, only a kind of elaborate party trick. If the non-naturalistic presentation of plays involves us in the action more than naturalistic theatre does, this is largely because it gives our imagination real work to do, which has the effect of making us want to contribute to the total event. Theatre is never just the play: it is always the play plus its audience.

This is not to suggest that naturalism itself fails to convince an audience that what is taking place is an authentic representation of life in terms of the theatre. Really lifelike presentation requires a very high degree of imagination from everyone involved in the play's production, in order to create a work of corporate art that calls from experience to experience across the gulf between two worlds. After all, the imaginative reconstruction of things that happen to us is part of the natural life of our emotions. By recognising our own history in the imaginative creations of other people we are reassured as to our own reality. Plays do not reproduce human life with all the accuracy of a video recorder in order to 'hold a mirror up to nature'; they do so by their ability to share, through the medium of artistic structure, images of experience that give rise to emotions that are authentically human, recognisably our own. The kind of theatre that Bertolt Brecht attacked when he spoke of the audience 'throwing itself into a play as if it were a river', was not particularly accurate in its portrayal of human mannerisms and ways of talking and moving, but its actors, directors and playwrights certainly aimed to seduce the audience into forgetting, while they were in the theatre, that that was actually where they were.

They did this by the realism of their ways of dealing with life. It was more important to convince emotionally than to persuade rationally, and a play was to be judged by the quality of the experiences it aroused, its emotional impact, rather than by the clarity of its message as something to be remembered and lived. Obviously the spectators' emotions would be engaged by the sight and sound of their fellow humans in situations of conflict and pain, trial and deliverance – but this should give weight to the play's argument and not obscure any kind of rational judgement about the value of its conclusions. It was obviously immoral to allow the villain of a play to arouse more sympathy than the hero. It is the responsibility of those who direct and act in plays to make sure that the opportunities for this kind of self-defeating (from the playwright's point of view) imaginative identification with all and sundry should not arise.[2]

Theatrical experience shows that the point is not proved. Attempts to control audience identification by editing the performance to produce an overall effect restricted to a particular point of view, that of either the playwright or the director, tend to backfire. There is something fundamental about the nature of theatre that makes its use for polemic impossible. In fact, this is one of the most interesting things about plays – that they have an effect upon audiences which cannot be assessed or understood in advance. The Brechtian experiment is a case in point. The more effort that is put into breaking the emotional tie between character and audience member, the stronger it becomes. To say that such relationships are *de facto* inappropriate because 'it is only a play' may seem a good way of undermining the powerful movement toward emotional involvement that exists in theatre but, as Denis Diderot (1957)[3] pointed out more than a century earlier, it fails to work. The knowledge that it is a play that we are watching tends always to make us participants, not critics. We are certainly aware during the performance of any shortcomings in the way things are being done on stage, and we may criticise to our hearts' content once the curtain has fallen and the stage lights gone out; in the play itself, however, enjoyment is conditional on a certain tolerance, a willingness to collude with the imitation of outward appearances and to condone its lack of total success.

Indeed, as Diderot says, the harder it is to believe that the stage world is what it says it is, the harder we try. Performances that are put together without any great skill or expertise, such as the children's nativity play in the church hall, are a good example of this. We do not weep simply because we are parents but because we find ourselves responding to the challenge of doing what we really want to do – reaching out to share this crudely constructed world with those whose natural universe it is: not the children who play the parts but the parts themselves, the crudely presented characters to whom they give life. The same kind of thing happens in the cinema, whose images are two-dimensional, transported to us by rays of light which we can actually see leaving the projection room on their journey across the darkened auditorium. We reach out to the artistically presented otherness, committing ourselves to personal encounter with the unknown, however terrifying may be the fictional situation we see before us on the screen. We know it cannot harm us, however. We are as safe in the horror movies as we are in the church hall.

---

2   cf Willett, J., The Theatre of Bertolt Brecht (London: Methuen, 1960).

3   1713–1784 (The Paradox of Acting was first published in 1830).

As we have seen in Chapter 1, it is because we are safe that we are able to put ourselves at risk. The invented nature of what is going on coaxes us out of our natural defensiveness. It does the same for the actor who stands terrified in the wings of the theatre, totally convinced that he will never dare set foot on the stage. The cue arrives and he is on-stage, put there by the character he is playing. The play's structure, by which we recognise it as a play and the theatre as a theatre, a place specifically designed for theatrical presentation, encourages us by its familiarity. We know what it is *for*, and we are not alarmed.

This is true even though the play itself and its presentation may actively seek to alarm us. No head-on attack on our sensibilities, however skilfully mounted, is likely to shake our position. We have come to suspend our disbelief and enjoy the experience. Devotees of horror movies recommend them precisely because of their failure to horrify: you know it isn't real, they say; you know you're quite safe. Films and plays which actually disturb us go about the job in an altogether less direct way, allowing us to frighten ourselves while retaining their own composure. The more obviously skilful – the more lifelike – the approach, the closer we cling to the knowledge that we are always quite safe because it is not actually true. Things that happen in theatres and cinemas are never true. Everybody knows that!

They may, however, be true *for us*. We may discover that on some level of awareness they refer to our condition. We may be reassured by the artificiality of an experience in which, one way or the other, we are never entirely unable to detect the joins in the scenery, and where the most lifelike presentation arouses our admiration principally because it *is* a presentation, rather than an ordinary, unrehearsed event; at the same time, the things that really reach us – move, touch, excite, delight, challenge, reassure, convict us – are the things that we discover for ourselves, the things that are not obvious, not plainly stated or 'handed to us on a plate'. For example, Shakespeare's striking use, in Hamlet and elsewhere, of the 'play within a play' reminds the audience of the contrived nature of plays in general, and his own in particular. Within the same tradition, Joan Littlewood urged her players to 'let the audience do the work.' The immense power of theatre is located not in the skilful imitation of life, either at acting or presentation level, but in the reality that people themselves bring, both as actors *and as audience*. This reality is discovered, not contrived. Presentation must be seen to be such or it will get in the way and distort the truth, which is always surprising, never expected. Truth happens in the gaps of the illusion – at the point where contrivance shows itself as itself. Because naturalistic presentation allows this to happen less obviously, and with less conviction that an intentionally theatrical approach, plays which say 'I am a play – this is what I say' are more effective communicators of the experience they embody than ones which simply say what they mean and leave it at that. Both message and meta-message – the message about the message, which says what kind of communicating method is being used – are essential for the suspension of disbelief. If we know it is a play, we work harder. We feel it is safe to do so.

It is this feeling of safety that allows us to identify with the people and happenings within the play – to take upon ourselves the emotional impact of the things we see acted out in our presence. Here again, dynamic psychology throws light on the nature of artistic experience. Patrick Casement describes a process of 'projective identification', as a result of which we project feelings that we ourselves cannot tolerate onto somebody else. Our sense of reality requires us to take account of such feelings – they *belong* to us – but we can only contemplate them when we have dissociated ourselves from our ownership of them. We may learn to do this very early on in our lives, even when we are still small children, according to Melanie Klein (Klein, 1946). However, it remains an unsatisfactory solution, both for ourselves and for the victims of our projections. 'What is needed', says Casement, 'is for the recipient, the mother or the therapist, to be more able to be in touch with these feelings than the infant or patient had been. When this response is found, the previously unmanageable feelings become more manageable.' (1985, 82). Manageable enough, that is, to be acknowledged and lived through.

In one of Casement's examples, he points out that 'it was the patient's own lack of emotion that had been having the greatest impact on me' (1985, 79). This was because this particular client had made the therapist feel 'what she herself could not bear to feel consciously within herself'. This seems particularly relevant to what happens in theatre, where *the nature of the theatrical content itself* permits the audience to feel secure in their imaginative involvement. Due to the fact that it is a play, we are able to take on the feelings projected by it and make them our own. They are, after all, the kinds of feeling we recognize from our own personal experience. Just as this patient's absence of obvious emotion made no demand, so that Casement found himself suffering on her behalf, so the emotions portrayed in our presence by those to whom they do not really 'belong', move us to tears. We carry the burden of pain on behalf of the play's characters, and it is the actors' job to let us do so. We shall be returning to the idea of theatre as a safe environment for the acknowledgement and transformation of feelings. It is crucial to the argument of this book, because it concerns the pre-conditions of theatrical catharsis.

For the time being, it is enough to acknowledge the fact that by allowing ourselves to believe in unreality we open ourselves to encounters with truth. When we stop protecting ourselves against any possible attempts to mislead and manipulate or to push us into positions of one kind or another, and, from a position of confidence, we qualify for genuine encounter, The work we do when we have reached such a position of existential confidence is our own work, freely undertaken in a spirit of responsiveness. We give ourselves to the action that unfolds before us, enfolding us in its beckoning life; but we do so because *we* choose, not because we are seduced by illusion, blackmailed by sympathy or directed how to react by a superior ideology. An underlying fact about theatre is that no-one responds to the order to direct his or her sympathies in one way rather than another. In fact, the opposite is true: we are much more likely to feel sorry for people in the play that we have been told to despise, and listen eagerly to characters whom the playwright or director instructs us to ignore. In fact the emotional effect of the techniques of 'alienation' that Brecht employs in order to detach the audience's sympa-thies from these stage personages with whom he does not want us to identify is quite considerable. If he makes them appear lifeless we immediately want to give them life; if he presents them as cruel and heartless we want to know how they came to be like that and whether, in certain circumstances, they might even be redeemable...

In fact, of course, to reveal the workings of the theatre to the audience is to increase their imaginative freedom and to undermine the usefulness of the drama as a political weapon designed to get across a particular set of arguments. To recognise the structure of the play's presentation is to understand what is happening – and to feel safe. In some circumstances, for some people, this might provide an opportunity to break off communications and turn thankfully aside from what might have been a terrifying encounter with the unknown. On the other hand, we are free to wonder why they chose to come to the theatre in the first place; the disbelief is suspended before they even buy a ticket! Probably, however, most of the audience are in another frame of mind and have come to the theatre to be entertained and 'taken out of themselves' in one way or another. Their reaction to the message 'relax, enjoy yourselves, it's only a play' is likely to be very different. Quite the opposite, in fact; the permission to relax encourages us to have the courage to be ourselves, and because we are human beings, our natural tendency is to identify with the people in the play, to feel their sorrows, share their joys, approve of their aims and tolerate their weaknesses. We shall do this because they remind us of ourselves and not because we are told to. Taking advantage of our special privileged position as audience members we try out a whole range of ideas and attitudes which are foreign to us, some with which we normally have sympathy and some which we would, in other circumstances, almost certainly find aversive. We do this freely, because we feel safe enough to take this kind of risk, because we are in a theatre. If, by any chance, the play goes out of its way to proclaim its fictional nature by letting us see behind the scenes and exaggerating its dramatic effects, we take advantage by investing our sympathies according to our impulse to identify, by becoming as many of the characters as we wish, as deeply as we wish.

Members of theatre audiences, conscious of the nature of the occasion and their own privileged identity, lower their defences in a way and to an extent that is unparalleled anywhere else. Outside the theatre they did not believe in what happens in plays and were surprised that you should think of asking such a question, wanting to know if you were mistaking them for children, perhaps? Once inside the building and sitting in their seats waiting for the house lights to dim, they would not even reply to such a question, being too busy preparing to concur with Coleridge and surrender to the imagination that they usually keep so well under control. Now this same imagination responds eagerly to the command to suspend disbelief and prepare to enter a new world where the passport for entry is an honest willingness to share whatever it is that is on offer. However celebrated the actors and actresses may be, the audience member is not a worshipper of any kind. He or she does not believe all the time, but only when the play is actually being performed. Looking back on it afterwards, it is necessary to recall not just the play, but the whole theatre; and when we do this we become aware of the true identity of the experience that we call theatre, which is always and inevitably not just the play, but *play plus setting* – in other words, the entire event.

Theatre is a global experience. Everything that takes place in this specially constructed alternative world is a vital part of the whole event. Using the language of root metaphors invented by Stephen Pepper (1942), we might say that the play itself is a 'contextual' image, and the theatre is its 'organismic' context – in other words, the stage action is a metaphor within a metaphor. To put this in another way, the play depends for its meaning and impact on the way in which it unfolds. It hangs together because of its plot, the specific way in which the story is organised for presentation. It is understood in retrospect, as different actions fall into place in the unfolding narrative. Contextual metaphors of life's meaning demonstrate the way in which human sense consists of the solution of problems that are experienced as insoluble before the answer to them has been revealed, and the episode becomes part of the way in which we organise the whole story.

The theatrical structure that permits such an unfolding to take place, by presenting the drama as a recognisable event, one which takes up several hours of our own as well as the actors' time, is also a metaphor. The root metaphor of theatre is spatial rather than temporal. It is a space that holds within itself an idea of temporal succession as this is depicted in and expressed by the living experiences of human beings. This requires much more than a machine, however complex. The organicist metaphor makes use of the idea of instrumentality but regards it as a form of human expressiveness. Consequently the theatre, designed to mirror the 'changes and chances of this mortal life' (The Book of Common Prayer) draws its imagery from living organisms and finds its principal value in expressiveness rather than machine-like efficiency. Rather, its skill lies in the representation of humanness and it functions in the way that organisms do by developing an overall effectiveness out-running analysis. The global nature of theatre originates in its identity as a holism, engaging the world in a range of interdependent ways and perpetually breaking new ground and so adding to its repertoire of human expressiveness. The encounter of self and other in which other becomes self is brought about by the orchestration of human ingenuity, as everyone involved in the theatrical enterprise, from theatre architect to call-boy, contributes to the massive corporate enterprise involved in allowing such a thing to happen on such a scale and with such clarity.

This, then, is the transitional corporate organism that is theatre. Play, safety and adventure here take place within a specially structured framework. It presents us with the actuality of human encounter in the circumstances of the greatest achievable mutuality, brought about in ways that are personal and technical. In theatre a mechanism is used to express personality, instead of persons being employed for any kind of instrumental or mechanistic purpose. The machinery of personal expressiveness inevitably takes on the identity of a living organism. The stage, the lighting, the music and its entire *mise en scéne*, as well as the technical plotting and experiment that belongs to every attempt at genuine human communication, are all extensions of human gesture; the actors themselves are the ambassadors of an entire world of experience that beckons us to share its life and our own. Theatre exemplifies the understanding of relationship which yields to experience rather than thought; or rather to the kind of thinking that is rooted in experience of the factual nature of people, objects and settings. It is a living demonstration of the way human consciousness belongs in the world it criticises, so that the human meaning is 'in' and 'from' as well as 'about' the reality to which it refers.

When we start to examine theatre as a functional organism directed towards relationship, we are immediately taken back to the circumstances in which human relationship itself originates – in other words to the dimensions of personal encounter which we looked at in the last chapter: separation and contact, safety and danger, focus and dispersed attention. We have seen that these are opposite ends of the same dimension, and that in each case the difference they express is one of degree rather than kind. Each pole of a mental construct suggests the other as well as being in contrast to it. New constructs come into being to express qualitative differences, not quantitative ones, which are perfectly adequately dealt with by the construct system as it stands. Whether we feel *more* or *less* separation, safety or focus, it remains separation, safety or focus that we feel; and it is the difference between any one of the three and anything else that we want to establish. We may talk or write or simply think about it, and use objects, places, colours, sounds, smells, tastes, movements, physical qualities to express it: in doing so we inevitably point to the whole range of intensities of which it is capable. More often than not we do not want to refer to the entire scope of a construct, but simply to identify something which occurs at some or other point within it. All the same, the principle remains – the presence of more always implies the existence of less, and vice versa.

Theatre, which goes to some lengths to demonstrate the separation of objects and people by proclaiming its own artificiality while appealing to human imagination, urging it to leap the gap between fiction and reality and give life to its well-rehearsed imitation, presents us with a paradigm rather than a paradox. The separation on which it depends belongs to the idea that it embodies. As we have seen, relationship is actually about separateness. Until we are aware of the latter how can we perceive any reality in the former? When theatre draws its line between actors and audience it is not a division between realities, but the division which characterises a single reality, that of personal relationship; and the way we make sense of it is not by using two separate ideas but by concentrating on the two poles of the same construct. In theatre we distance ourselves in order to be engaged with whatever we are standing back from. The action of distancing is, in fact, not an obstacle to be overcome. It *is* the relational act.

At this point we are led to quote from Rollo May's wonderful book, *The Courage to Create*:

> 'Cezanne sees a tree. He experiences, as he would no doubt have said, "being grasped by the tree". The arching grandeur of the tree, the mothering spread, the delicate balance as the tree grips the earth – all these and many more characteristics of the tree are absorbed

into his perception and are felt through his nervous structure... This vision involves an omission of some aspects of the scene and a greater emphasis on other aspects and the ensuing re-arrangement of the whole; but it is more than the sum of all these. Primarily it is a vision that is not now tree but Tree; the concrete tree that Cezanne looked at is formed into the essence of tree. However original and unrepeatable his vision is, it is still a vision of all trees triggered by his encounter with this particular one.' (1975; 77,8)

We may use the word 'encounter' loosely in common speech in order to express all kinds of human and non-human contact, including our experience of things within the natural world. Here, however, it has a special meaning, referring to the way in which an artist distances him or herself from whatever it is that must be reproduced as a work of art, something that manages to retain enough of its original being to express itself in another medium. The relationship between Cezanne and the tree is not interrupted by the change, although it involves a radical break in form, substance, location. The continuity of the engagement establishes the nature of relationship itself. The awareness of separation from another being – even another kind of being – holds us together in a loving unity.

The dimension of separation/contact is clearly revealed by a work of art. The presence of danger/safety is not so obvious at first, until we realise that the tree's true being, experienced as a radical otherness, is an intractable refusal to be caught within a web of romantic, tragic or merely sentimental ideas about trees, thus reducing it to some kind of cultural icon rather than the expression of treeness, independent and unbowed. To fight against one's own ideas and feelings about trees when painting one is to be willing to take a step in the dark; to trust to the subject itself for enlightenment is an attitude of mind which requires a good deal of deconstructive effort and a fair degree of the 'courage to be'. What will I be left with when I have abandoned the safety of familiar images and well-tried techniques? Only the love that casts out fear, which is the essence of relationship. Seen in this light, suspension of disbelief is revealed as the primary gesture of theatrical encounter; to suspend disbelief is to overcome the impulse of defensiveness and take the first step towards the other. This takes some courage, because the circumstances are fantasy; but the meeting is recognised, for better or worse, as personal.

As we have seen, the purpose of the experience of a shared fantasy that we call 'going to the theatre' is to promote genuine encounter of selves and the understanding and acceptance of self and other to which encounter gives rise. (Two of the primary meanings of 'entertain' are, according to the *Oxford*

English Dictionary, 'welcome' and 'support' – and yet we talk about 'mere entertainment'![4]) It may seem strange that such truth should emerge from an obvious fantasy, but such is the relationship-producing force of the transitional object. As often as we enjoy our fantasies in private, we use them to found relationship. The best example of this is the process of falling in love. This kind of personal commitment must be wholehearted; again, our acceptance of the theatrical invitation is a willing one, and we focus all our attention upon the world of the play, excluding everything else from our line of sight so as not to be distracted from our purpose.

The kinds of art in which ideas and feelings are embodied within our own psychosomatic identity – our actual physical presence – depend on a high degree of concentration upon their subject matter. As we shall see, actors perform precise and deliberate techniques, disciplining themselves to dissociate from their 'core roles' as actors and actresses, the ways in which they are accustomed to seeing themselves, in order to step aside into someone else's identity and 'lose themselves' in the parts they are playing. To perform such a transfer of role is, of course, to take on an entirely new frame of reference. Obviously one needs to be very sure about what it is that one is losing oneself in, and where it is situated with regard to oneself. The process of developing a stage character is that of elaborating a new way of looking at reality, taking on a new personal construct system. The more elaborate the system, the more real the 'new' person for the actor. The actor's sense of identity in his or her new role communicates itself to each person in the audience; but only if the audience member is willing to entertain it, to bestow on it the blessing of some kind of personal acceptance. By accepting we bestow; the process is one of an interchange of being, something that requires concentration and a sense of purpose, of being committed to our engagement with a particular person or group of people.

In the theatre this process is assisted by various ways of focusing attention on our new world. On the one hand are things that remind us of the normal procedures of human recognition such as sounds, shapes, colours, sensory reminders of the familiar world outside the theatre; on the other are things aimed at making the image harder to avoid by giving it depth and sharpness, multi-dimensionality and solidity; sensually exciting experiences that draw us out of ourselves, distracting us from our normal preoccupations, making us forget the circumstances that inhibit our surrender to the object of our

---

4   cf Shakespeare, W. *Henry V*, Act V scene iv:
     'Now entertain conjecture of a time
     When creeping murmur and the poring dark
     Fills the wide vessel of the universe.'

attention. The theatre's manipulation of the visual, aural and kinetic dislodges us from the way in which we customarily perceive the things of life, and in doing so it loosens our grasp on what these things habitually mean to us, the interpretation that we are accustomed to give them. Theatre uses a whole range of techniques to dislodge us from our preoccupation with the reality we have just left behind by transforming our sense of what is going on around us. The most important way of all, however, is the theatrical use of focus, what we normally call theatrical or dramatic *distance*.

This is a very important concept which we will be discussing in the following chapter. The new social frame or dramatic world into which we are invited when we enter a theatre takes visible and aural form in the arrangements specially made for our arrival. The thing to notice at this point is that we are both challenged and reassured by the new world that confronts us. It is both familiar and strange. Here, strangeness and familiarity interact, confirming and contradicting one another at different levels. On one level of awareness, the strangeness is a source of comfort. This is not our world, our life, but a fictional scenario. This of course is the primary dramatic level; but we are asked to suspend this kind of disbelief and to enter into things as if they were part of ordinary everyday reality. Here again, there is a conflict between safety and danger, as we are reassured by the details of human life with which we are familiar, and troubled by being reminded of our personal anxieties and preoccupations. More important than these, although obviously connected with them, is the challenge of identification, as we find ourselves drawn into personal relationships of sympathy and empathy equally rooted in the projection of our own personal reality, our selfhood, into the lives of other people; putting ourselves on the line through the power of our imagination which implicates us in lives which are not our own. So we find ourselves back at the beginning, accused by belonging to the human race, acquitted on the plea of mistaken identity.

These things happen to us because we have agreed to co-operate, and because the theatrical organism, once having got hold of us, focuses us in such a way as to transform co-operation into collusion, making sure that courage and confidence overcome the impulse of self-protectiveness and unwillingness to become involved. In the conflict between safety and danger, safety triumphs to the extent that more and more dangerous areas are made secure for exploration. Having established this pole of the construct in a convincing way, we can experiment with the balance between danger and safety, and perhaps even shift the position of the fulcrum on which it rests. Although the terms of reference may be as wide as imagination itself, theatre tackles life by a process of focused imagination whose purpose is to establish a position of temporary existential confidence which acts as a launching pad for discovering new ways of relating to the world and re-discovering ones that have been overlaid or forgotten. In order to do this it adopts a strategy of 'divide and rule' in its selection of subject matter as well as actual presentation of plays. Literally and metaphorically we are directed where to look. Burns describes 'the process of confining attention to those involved in a specific situation, (and) of limiting activities...to what is appropriate, or meaningful, or consequential and observing a defined level of reality' (1972, 17). In this and other ways our natural fears, as well as our more neurotic anxieties, are contained so that they can be put to creative use as part of the honesty and wholeheartedness of our gesture towards the other.

The notion of personal honesty, of the candid admission of human vulnerability, is fundamental to Coleridge's doctrine. Disbelief is suspended rather than abandoned. To abandon it altogether in such circumstances would be, to say the least, foolhardy. Our secondary identification, in which we abandoned our dependence on the satisfactions of private fantasy for the maturer joys of social belonging, was not achieved so easily that we can afford to lose our grasp on public reality except in very special circumstances. Except in public, that is, and for fun. The prospect of playing a game is always attractive, because it means working to a new set of rules, which in itself implies that other kinds of regulation are relaxed during the time and in the place specially set aside for the purpose. The main de-regulation is that concerning the hold that must be exerted, under normal social circumstances, upon the imagination. Because they are played to special rules, all games are licensed fantasy. We know this very well, or course – which is why we are willing to relax our hold on the world outside and concentrate, for the time being, on the game. The world is still there; indeed, it is the world of human interaction and psychosomatic presence, that provides the setting for our fantasy games, allowing us to say 'Stop! This far and no further! Be suspended.' Suspension of disbelief says quite clearly that the rule of fantasy is limited and circumscribed by an understanding of social reality which is never fully abandoned, and which is able to incorporate the results of these special dramatic excursions in to 'as if' within its own undisputed territory.

CHAPTER 4

Role

In the Introduction we wrote that the audience shares with the actor the 'gift of the self'. What we have said up to now shows that we feel this to be crucial to an understanding of what happens in theatre. It is, in other words, as close to the definition of the theatrical act as we can come. It is impossible to say which makes the greater contribution to the sharing because it is essentially an experience of reciprocal acceptance, an encounter which renounces dialogues of dominance or manipulation; which sees them and sees through them in order to achieve a special kind of mutuality. At the same time, however, the actor plays an instrumental part as the one who initiates the crucial transaction, who makes the welcoming gesture on which the relationship is to be built. This gesture, the invitation to enter into a temporarily shared reality, takes place within and through the context of the role that the actor inhabits. Without characters, there can be no drama.

Here, we shall explore role in its social and theatrical contexts, and see how each illuminates and is illuminated by the other. We feel that is important to make the distinction between role and character, though the terms are often used almost interchangeably. We see the role as 'one's function, what one is appointed or expected or has undertaken to do' (Concise Oxford Dictionary) and the character as the collection of qualities, attitudes and beliefs which are unique to an individual person or personage. We believe that this distinction is important, and will elaborate on it in due course.

There is no stage in life where we do not occupy at least one role, whether consciously or not. Even the infant in utero can be said to be offstage; the audience is aware of their imminent appearance. Though the newborn is not able to be aware of him or herself in differentiated role, we as parents, siblings or interested onlookers are very much aware of his or her role as newcomer. As we grow and develop, we acquire a changing set of roles. The developmental processes of individuation and projective identification that we have described enable us to become aware not only of the self but of the self as being in role. This awareness extends to that of the other-in-role, and of all the interactions and relationships between the self-in-role and others-in-role. As part of this process, we develop the capacity for cathexis; the imbuing of the inanimate with feelings and human qualities – the creation of the transitional object. These objects are initially receptacles for our potentially destructive anger at separation and are also symbolic of the mother-who-will-return, and they naturally become decathected with the passage of time; yet the capacity remains with us and is a significant part of our ability to engage in drama. The projection of emotion onto the transitional object is, if you like, the first instance of the suspension of disbelief. In adulthood this suspension does not only relate to living actors upon the stage; it also relates to the animated character in the dramatic forms of puppetry and the cartoon. Tom and Jerry act out our destructive fantasies for us, and cannot themselves be destroyed. The phenomenon of cathexis also lives on in social reality, as we not only give the objects around us emotional significance as status symbols or cherished keepsakes – we also attribute motivations and conscious behaviours to them. When we laugh at John Cleese in the role of Basil Fawlty belabouring his recalcitrant car, we are not so much laughing at his absurdity, but in recognition of our own.

Roles enable us to name the boundaries of me and not-me; I am the child and you are my mother. They give us a clear sense of our place within the vast and complex social network and bring understandable order to what would otherwise be undifferentiated chaos. However, though our roles serve to delineate our boundaries, they are not us and we are not them. We are far more than the sum of our role-set. A role is, in effect, a potential space to be moved into, to inhabit; the social or personal role is a space inhabited by the self. The boundaries of our roles touch the boundaries of others' roles and thus form an interface that we experience as relationship, filtering that experience through the mesh of our expectations of others, their expectations of us and our own expectations of the self-in-role. We enact our roles uniquely by suffusing them with our own character and selfhood.

Kielhofner (1985), looking at role from an occupational perspective, identifies the expectations of self and society which are placed upon a role; internal and external expectations. He describes 'perceived incumbency'; the sense of how much one has the right to inhabit a particular role and how effectively one perceives oneself enacting it. He also refers to 'role balance', which is the acquisition of an optimal repertoire of roles which tend to work synergistically rather that antagonistically. He outlines the set of occupational roles (those which pertain to or support functional and purposeful behaviour) as being *student, worker, volunteer, care giver, home maintainer, friend, family member, religious participant, amateur/hobbyist and participant in an organization* (1985, 26). It can be seen that these are potentially functional or positive roles, and he also acknowledges the presence of deviant or dysfunctional roles which 'are seen by society as diverging from normal behaviour' (1985, 26), such as the sick role, or the invalid. For example, the etymology of the word invalid suggests that such a person cannot fully validate themselves within society by virtue of their disability or illness. He feels that 'roles serve as backdrops that influence how one behaves and experiences one's own and other persons' behaviour.' (1985, 27)

Goffman (1990) presents us with a dramaturgical model of society, in which there are three 'crucial roles'; those of *Performer, Audience and Outsiders*. He delineates the regions to which the various role players have access; the front region and the back region. These regions are the social equivalent of onstage and backstage. The performers have access to both front and back regions, the audience to the front region only and the outsiders to neither. This is an appealing model of social role play as it is easy for us to identify with the cosy informality of the back region and the self-consciousness of the front region as well as the feelings of awkwardness when a member of the social audience penetrates backstage, or an outsider enters the social drama. However, we feel that Goffman is in danger of oversimplifying the case. It cannot be denied that there are the social equivalents of on and offstage and that we act differently in those regions, but nevertheless, we *act*. Whenever two or more people are together, there is always a performer or performers, and there is always an audience. Even when we are alone, there is the potential audience that may at any moment arrive to witness us. There is also the immanent audience for those who believe in God; our actions, if He exists, are by definition always witnessed. In any case, we often act as audience to our own actions in moments of self consciousness or self awareness. It may only be when we are asleep that we are truly offstage, and even then, if we are sleeping in the presence of a waking partner, then we are still onstage, if not consciously so as a performer.

Here, we begin to touch on the concept of awareness of being in role. For most of our waking hours, perhaps, we play our roles naturally and spontaneously. The social drama is experienced as a seamless matrix of action and interaction where figure and ground are in constant flux; where actors and audience are one. And yet there are moments when we suddenly become acutely conscious of ourselves-in-role. We would postulate that this will tend to occur in quite specific circumstances. When a role is new to us, we inevitably have a heightened awareness of our performance in role. The pattern of behaviours and interactions has not yet become habitual. If our sense of perceived incumbency in a particular role is weak (which could be through newness in role, but could also be from a longer standing lack of faith in the self-in-role), we are again acutely aware of just how we are acting in role. In the case of a role which is normally enacted fluently and with confidence, a new or particularly demanding situation will tend to evoke an awareness of enacting our role carefully and deliberately to ensure that our performance is at its most effective. This perhaps implies that for the eventual successful performance of each role, there is also a corresponding rehearsal period, where we are fully aware of the quality of our performance in role; self-conscious, in fact. As we become more accomplished performers, we lose the internal dialogue (which is analogous to Stanislavski's internal critic) in which we reflect on our performance and gradually refine it. Our actions in role become more spontaneous and need less or no rehearsal precisely because we have established the dramatic safety net which allows that spontaneity. The ritual which allows the taking of risks which Jennings describes in reference to dramatherapy is also a necessary part of our social existence.

The accommodation period to a new role need not only be notional; society may give it formal recognition. A newcomer to a particular milieu is given an unspoken period to acclimatize themselves to the group norms, to the rules of that particular social game, which are a close analogue to the dramatic text in terms of scripts and stage directions at least. In employment based roles, this may be the overt and formalized process of induction training and the probationary period. In those relationships where two people are contemplating a long term commitment to their partnership a lot of the rehearsal occurs in the courtship period, and the relationship may be ritually formalized by marriage, which not only marks, but also facilitates the transition from one role to another. Throughout life, we will inevitably be startled into awareness of ourselves-in-role by the unexpected. It is important for us to recognize that this awareness is not necessarily the discomfort of self-consciousness but can also be an awareness of enacting a role as skillfully as we can, with an accompanying sense of self-validation and existential joy.

Here, it would seem, we have a continuum of awareness of the self-in-role. This does not exist in isolation; it acts on and is modified by other continua. Goffman (1990) identified belief or lack of belief in the role being enacted (on the part of the audience) and sincerity or cynicism in role (on the part of the actor). We would add further continua to the picture. There is the level of complexity of a role; some roles can be briefly sketched in to make them viable and others carry an almost unimaginable weight of history and social complexity. There is the degree of rigidity or flexibility that requires some roles to be enacted to a set of strict definitions and allows others to be interpreted far more liberally. A typical example of a highly structured social role is that of royalty, and it is interesting to note that individuals who decide to introduce more flexibility or spontaneity to the way that they enact such a role may find that in doing so, the original role becomes untenable, or that other players in the drama may attempt to eject them from their role. Antigone (Anouilh, 1951) finds herself forced into making a choice between remaining in role as Creon's dutiful niece (thereby denying her brothers their funeral rites) or extending her role in order to act congruently with her sense of what is right (thereby breaking the law). Throughout Anouilh's play, the various members of her family plead and attempt to browbeat her into remaining in role. Eventually, she consciously rejects this role which has become untenable for her. The only way that Creon can deal with this is to order her death; the ultimate way of ensuring that her role remains forever immutable. Once she is dead Antigone can no longer change.

Clinical experience gives us the example of the individual who seeks to change the way that they play their own life roles, perhaps through assertiveness training. They often meet with powerful opposition from those in their social milieu who have a vested interest in maintaining the original passive character. Refusal to be thus coerced can lead to irretrievable breakdown in existing relationships. There is also the continuum of skill-clumsiness, where a role is enacted more or less adeptly. This continuum does not necessarily parallel that of the audience's continuum of belief-disbelief; we may believe absolutely in the sincerity of the clumsy lover and see through the cynicism of the skilled seducer. Fundamental to all of the above continua is that of engagement–disengagement; the degree to which we are actually involved with or distanced from our role. This is perhaps the most significant of the group in terms of social and theatrical reality. As we have said, a role is a potential space which can be moved into by an individual. We can move into that space and fill it with the self, even push its boundaries out to extend and develop the role. On the other hand, we may enter the space tentatively, dipping our toes into it but never filling it with the potentiality of the self. Landy (1993, 25) refers to Scheff's concept of aesthetic distance, overdistance and underdistance and looks at this in terms of individuals being over or underdistanced from their roles. Perhaps a final continuum is that of fixity–fluidity by which we are more or less able to move from one role to another. Some individuals have the happy gift of moving smoothly from one role to another; others flop about like fish out of water when thrust into an unfamiliar role context. It is often more devastating to an individual to lose a primary role – as parent, spouse, worker, wage-earner, for example – than to lose a person they love; loss of role is experienced as loss of the self as familiar boundaries are ripped away.

The concept of a somehow fixed set of roles which make up the human repertoire is seductive. It carries within itself the satisfaction of completion; this is the set of roles available to us, that can be studied and understood. Now we know where and what we are. Goffman has his three 'crucial' roles, and elaborates on them with the introduction of 'discrepant' roles where the role player is not what he initially seems to be. One example that he uses is that of the 'shill'; the con-artist's accomplice who appears to be part of the audience but is in covert alliance with the performer. Those discrepant roles, however, do not actually extend the performer–audience–outsider triad; they are variations on a theme. Kielhofner gives us the set of ten occupational roles that we have referred to. He places those roles firmly within the internal context of the motivations, routines and skills which sustain them, and also within the external context of the physical and social environments in which they are enacted. Landy (1993) takes the process of naming roles much further. In his exploration of the origins of role, he comes to the conclusion that throughout the history of the dramatic text specific characters may change according to the social and cultural context of the time, but the essential role-types remain similar. He shows how these role-types are modified by their qualities, their functions and the style in which they are enacted. In an exhaustive trawl through theatrical texts, he distils out his taxonomy of roles which encompasses 84 types and further subtypes, which he classifies according to the overriding domains of the somatic, the cognitive, the affective, the social and the spiritual. Although his approach, on the surface, may appear to be nominalistic and reductionist, he places the roles held by individuals within a systemic context which transforms his model. It is not enough simply to list the roles which we are capable of enacting. Roles only take on their full significance when seen as interactional entities. In role, we necessarily interact with the physical and social environment which we inhabit, and our interactions and experience of those interactions are modified by those environments.

It is logical thus to view individuals and their interactions within society in theatrical terms. It is precisely our capacity as role playing creatures that has given rise to theatre itself. We are fascinated by ourselves as individuals in role, and yet we can never fully appreciate ourselves in the moment of performance. As Wilshire points out, we can never completely see ourselves except as reflected in a mirror. This is true in actuality; the only way that one can examine all of the external self is by using at least two reflecting surfaces placed at angles to one another. The way that we perceive ourselves socially is through the mirror of others' reactions to us. Shakespeare, of course, recognised this: Cassius, though admittedly acting through self-interest rather than altruism, makes this offer to Brutus: 'And since you know you cannot see yourself So well as by reflection, I, your glass, Will modestly discover to yourself That of yourself which you yet know not of' (*Julius Caesar*, Act I, scene ii). We are the reflecting surfaces for one another, and as Wilshire says: 'What if a life is a human life because it is mediated by communal fantasy and belief about everyday life, and theatre and other arts articulate and consummate this mediation?' (1982, 3–4). In other words, theatre holds up a mirror to human life.

Unlike everyday life, however, theatre is a selective mirror. The theatrical role, as Wilshire shows us (1982, 21), differs from social roles in that it is deliberately enacted before an audience within the context of an acknowledged performance that is time-limited and capable of being repeated. It enables the audience to separate figure from background in a way that is not so possible in life. The experience of the social milieu and the self as social agent is so packed with stimuli that our attention can never focus on the whole picture; figure and ground become blurred and we cannot see the wood for the trees. Through standing in for a personage and enacting the role in a certain way and context, the actor is able to clarify the picture for us. The world is illuminated for us and the significant stands out in sharp relief. Wilshire's view is that theatre itself enables us to understand ourselves as individuals and as social creatures. It is much more than the social model proposed by Goffman, which enables sense to be made of social phenomena from the stand-point of a non-participant observer; here, the distance between observer and observed is startlingly different from that between actor and audience. It is only in the theatrical interchange that the willing suspension of belief acts directly upon the relationship. It is precisely this which enables us to look with courage into the theatrical mirror.

CHAPTER 5

Catharsis and 'As If'

The unique quality of the world of drama, the stage world, is the ability to challenge and reassure at the same time. At one level of our awareness it is the strangeness itself, the inescapable suggestion of a charade, the knowledge that however convincing they may be, people are *acting* that reassures us. This is something very like our world, but it is obviously not that world but a made up one, in which the joys and sorrows, problems and solutions are not ours, but belong to a group of personages who do not really exist. To suspend our disbelief is to lay these considerations aside, but not before we have recognised the presence of things that remind us forcibly of the anxiety that subsists in being human. Somehow the presence of those structured elements on which the performance depends does not finally convince us that it is, in fact, more unreal than real. The list of these evidences of human ingenuity is a considerable one, including such things as costume; make up; stage settings; lighting and sound effects; music and dance, or other kinds of stylized movement; masks and cultic objects – all of which have the ambiguous effect of communicating an atmosphere of strangeness in a language with which we are all more or less familiar. The ambiguity adds to the special nature of the occasion, as we ask ourselves questions as to the nature of the proceedings knowing full well the answer. Fantasy and reality set the scene for what is about to happen here. What we are accustomed to think of as opposites, reveal themselves as the two extremes of the same dimension of human experience – that which concerns the intensity of our other-awareness. Are we meeting or hiding? If we are hiding, why are we going about it in this peculiar fashion, going to these outrageous lengths to communicate our non-communication? In other words, why are we making such a show of it?

This mixture of worlds is one way of making contact with individual human beings at a level of understanding which allows them to rediscover for themselves the relationship between separation and mutuality as one of continuity, in which the one leads into the other rather than simply interrupting or negating it. As we have seen, one pole of a construct requires the other; we cannot avoid defining things by their opposites. By entering a world of obvious make-believe we are inevitably reminded about truth; the illusion of theatre brings us face to face with our own reality. After all, it is not straightforward artificiality that confronts us but an imaginative self-expression, a demonstration of human possibility in terms of actual bodily presences and identifiable human situations. We feel drawn to associate ourselves with what we recognise as authentically human. The fact that it is clothed in the ingenuity of a fictional plot makes our need to intervene even more pressing than ever; we want to rescue it for truth, our own truth.

The stage world, then, employs human ingenuity to involve us in its action so that we may share its experience. Our attention is focused on a special privileged area, painstakingly set apart for our scrutiny, in the hope that its obvious artificiality will induce us to play at believing in it. The intricate structures involved in doing so fascinate us by their ability to be true and false, disarming and challenging at the same time, and we strive to make them wholly true, wholly identifiable in terms of personal reality. I have written elsewhere that

> 'The audience is at one and the same time protected and exposed – protected by the fictional or metaphoric structure of the event, exposed by the hypnotic fascination of the theatrical image, which is focused and intensified by the very things that seem to set it apart from life and render it harmless. The artistic nature of the happening distinguishes two separate but mutually inclusive worlds brought into relationship by a line of demarcation which unites what it divides.' (Grainger, 1990, 19)

This crucial 'line of demarcation' is the space between audience and actors, the element of structure which defines and determines the nature of everything that will take place within the theatrical event, the most important structural factor of all. The physical separation of audience and actors, *theatron* and *skene*, is in itself the pivotal structural element, and as such, it is crucial to the way that the organism functions. It is the spatial form assumed by the psycho-spiritual phenomenon of aesthetic distance which marks theatre as the living demonstration of the dynamism of the human relationship.

Creativity arises out of the tension between spontaneity and limitations (May, 1975, 115). We find ourselves recapitulating what we said in Chapter 1 about the fundamental character of human encounter as this is so very vividly described by Martin Buber: 'I–Thou', which stands for human involvement with the other, continually becomes 'I–It', as human awareness itself is a movement away from engagement prior to the action of re-engaging. Human consciousness moves back and forth, to and from the object of experience, preserving the independence of that object against confusion with and incorporation in the self, and reasserting the self's integrity in the wake of its global experience of the object. The movement between I–Thou and I–It and back again is both self-preserving and self-sacrificing, as we lose and find ourselves in a relationship which confirms us as beings both distinct from and totally involved in what is not ourself.

For this to happen we must continually adjust the ways in which we regard ourselves and other people, setting up interpersonal situations in which the awareness of self and other is kept continually alive. This is not simply a matter of the ways we think about or interpret life, or even the way we experience the presence of other people; it concerns the kinds of social situations we find ourselves in and the ways in which these are staged. We experience the presence of our next-door neighbours differently from opposite sides of the garden fence from the way in which we feel towards them when we are having a drink in the same bar – and this is not only because of the effect of alcohol. What Moreno referred to as socio-dramatic values – where and how people are sitting and standing, kneeling or lying down, the actual physical juxtaposition of bodies within the same space and the division of social space using articles of furniture or fixed barriers of some kind – are factors of tremendous importance in our social arrangements, always influencing and sometimes actually dictating the kind of encounter that takes place. It is the image of such encounters with others that determines the quality of our relationship to them. The meeting of persons not only requires the structure of things, it also reflects that structure.

Nowhere is this more clearly demonstrated than in the theatre building itself, where interior shape is designed specially to facilitate the kind of personal encounter that we have been describing. In his essay on the staging of the Greek tragic theatre, Buber suggests that the presence of a space between *theatron* and *skene* in the amphitheatres of classical Greece contributed powerfully to the intensity of the relationship which developed between actors and audience, upon which the phenomenology of identification depends. The theatre organism's use of aesthetic distance embodied in the actual space between audience and actor is the key to its function, just as the aesthetic distance provided by his or her dramatic role is the means of identification between actor and stage personage, and also between actor and actor, role and role. All these relationships come into being for human encounter symbolised by the actual physical distance between audience and acting area. This is the world between worlds, the setting for a series of interdependent and mutually validating alliances which make theatre the place of a living dream. In these encounters, a whole series of 'as ifs' are made the assertion of a single truth by their presentation in terms of an over-arching symbolism of encounter.

Aesthetic distance, says Wilshire, 'regulates the intercourse of 'world' (the world of the play) and world.' His next words strike to the heart of the matter: 'It is just because of this protection that the audience can uncover itself at its most vulnerable levels: its archaic mimetic fusions with others' (1982, 23). As we have seen, this fusion-in-separation is characteristic not only of the cultural way of perceiving human reality but of the emergence of personhood in individual people as a crucial stage in the awareness of each growing child. Theatre is a place that reminds us of our real identity by reproducing the conditions under which we became people. At the same time, there is no doubt at all of the venerable role it plays within human culture. In his essay on the staging of classical Greek tragedy, Buber suggests that the actual shape of the Greek amphitheatres made a vital contribution to the identification which took place between actor and audience by interposing a vast median territory in which the two worlds could be seen as meeting without any loss of identity. He describes the theatrical event as one subsisting in a 'polarity of familiarity and strangeness, total enjoyment and total renunciation' (1957, 67) according to which the willing gift of the self is the gesture that creates our own identity. In Greek theatre, we are united with ourselves by 'the stern overagainstness of I and Thou' (1957, 66) reaching across in fellowship to what is not ourself but calls out to us for recognition and acceptance, validation, love.

Although this book is mainly concerned with theatre rather than religious ritual, attention must be drawn here to the shared ground which exists between the two. There are obvious differences. Theatre does not have to concern itself with the proclamation of a religious message; the parts played are those of members of human social groups, human beings not gods nor a mixture of the two categories. The audience's involvement is understood to be optional rather than in any sense compulsory for the attainment of authentic human-ness. Most important of all, the focus of encounter is between human beings rather than human being and divinity. Consequently, in corporate ritual, aesthetic distance occurs elsewhere. Rites are designed with the line of demarcation *on the other side of the human group* rather than cutting across it, so that the worshipping community are conscious of reaching out to an Other who is beyond as well as between, although it is understood as transcendent. The means employed to contact this are the same, however. The medium of personal encounter is always the same willingness to give and receive life, the spirit of mutuality between persons. In rite and theatre a space is cleared for this meeting – for the life that moves between self and other. This special place is the power-house of the whole event, the source of all the changes that happen as a result of it. Ritual is very clear about what such changes are – no less than the importation of divinity into the lives of men and women. Rites of passage, which signify and implement important changes in the lives of individuals, groups and entire societies, influence personal and social history in the direction of a superior way of existing. This is brought about symbolically by a process of unmaking and re-making that takes place in the rite's central 'movement' the 'time out of time' which is so meticulously staged in the specially prepared ritual ground. The rite itself is divided into three parts in order to embody the shape of genuine existential change. Real change is never a smooth transition from 'before' to 'after', (which is the way in which we usually prefer to think of it, conveniently omitting the actual change itself, the painful immediacy that is neither before nor after), but only *now*. Until this is registered, nothing has really changed at all. Rites of passage provide us with no way of avoiding the actuality of change. In the complete 'passage ritual complex' the central liminal ritual is preceded by a rite of 'pre-liminal separation' and followed by one of 'post-liminal incorporation'. The impact of these three ritual stages is to bring home the action of a complete event in a way that will establish it as a turning point in life for those concerned.

The entire complex depends on what takes place in the median phase of the central ritual (Gennep, 1960). In this spiritually privileged geographical location, the neophyte or person to be initiated is subjected to experiences designed to destroy the structure of his or her expectations and interpreta-tions of life so that within her or him, too, a space may be cleared for new life to take possession. In order for such a total removal to take place, the old fabric of life must have been rendered totally uninhabitable. A study of religious rituals reveals the fact that ritual itself embodies the same kind of progression 'from lower to higher ground'. Everywhere, the three-fold shape of ritual reproduces the form of personal transformation. Every ritual is a rite of passage, whether or not it plays a part in the official structure of society. It does so by concentrating its efforts on the 'time between', the operative ritual movement which holds past and future apart; this is the catalyst that permits a human transformation while preserving the integrity of a personal history. These are things that happened to me, causing me to be as I am.

In fact, real personal change always happens in three stages, and the central stage is always the crucial one. For the new personal world to emerge, the old state of affairs must necessarily have been ended in a way that is psychologically and spiritually satisfactory to the individual. Memories are one thing – loose ends, unfinished business, is quite another. In rites of passage the future is severed from the past by an episode of radical discontinuity which always disturbs and often frightens those subject to it. In every religious ritual, but most strikingly in passage rites, the contact with other is presented in such a radical and uncompromising way. Thus the establishment of a new situation which is finally and completely dissociated from the limitations and imperfections of the past depends on the survival of the trauma of an event capable of shattering our equanimity to such a degree that we are cut completely adrift from our existential moorings and thrust into an ocean of fears and inadequacies, a turmoil of existential chaos reflecting the one that the rite has managed to reproduce in the ritual drama of its central phase.

This sounds considerably more terrifying than it actually is. Anthropologists such as Viktor Turner (1974) and Gilbert Lewis (1980), while not understating the fears of the neophytes caught up in the ritual scenario, point out that even the unexpected and terrifying may be supportable if there are others equally outfaced and even humiliated; while the powerful assurance that whatever happens in the ritual place, however punitive and rejecting it may seem to be, *must be intentional* – that it must serve the purposes of people and gods who have been shown to have their real welfare at heart – operates at a deeper level of awareness than psychological disorientation, fitting even the a-contextual into a kind of context. To encounter the other in whatever form it, he or she may take is not an experience that can be planned. Certainly the scene may be set for it, as happens in drama and ritual. However, it is an event which creates structure but itself continues to escape it. There is in fact an important practical purpose for physical and mental pain inflicted on candidates on the rite's central phase: to distract them from the more terrifying prospect of the most radical and salutary of all encounters, that with Otherness itself.

In religious mythologies throughout the world – and indeed in developed religions themselves – this central ritual ground is represented as the place of theophany, the meeting place of heaven and earth, eternity and time, mankind and divinity. Within the myth the point at which this life-giving contact occurs may be a tree joining earth to heaven as in shamanistic religions, a well or a cave symbolising the womb of life or the navel at which human life is eternally joined to its divine source, as in the Greek *omphaloi*.

The first suggests union with a god who lives in the heavens, the other two point to an earth goddess as the original cause and matrix of human being. In both cases, however, the identity of the symbol as a *coincidenta oppositorum*, the union of opposites, is most strikingly salient; both communicate connection and separation, as human and divine occupy the same axis, joined as the opposing poles of a single construct are always joined. The religious union of wholeness is typically that of the reconciliation of opposites which outside the religious dimension would be impossible. The archetypal image of the *mandala*, in which the miraculous coming together of inverse values is represented by 'squaring the circle', finds a series of geographical locations in holy places through out the world (Jung, 1938; McGuire and Hull, 1978). For instance, the Australian 'alcheringa' or 'dream time' is both a state of consciousness and the special dancing ground in which this is experienced. Above all, the sacred space is the spatio/temporal location of our encounter with the science of personhood. In these special circumstances, 'The dimension of the divine…is opened on the basis of the human face' (Levinas, 1969, quoted in Derrida, 1987, 145).

Buber states that it is essentially the same phenomenon that takes place in theatre. Divinity, as meaning, purpose, direction, growth, life, spirit, happens between persons in a relation localised 'not in individual souls, or in a generalised world which embraces and determines them, but in actual fact *between* them' (1961, 244). There is an essential relationship between the self and God which is to be understood as every experience of reaching out, or across, to another person. In our availability to know other people as themselves, we know God as himself; in turning to the others, 'being is disclosed to us', for 'every particular Thou is a glimpse through to the eternal Thou' (1966, 40, 75). Seen from this angle, every theatre becomes a church, a place in which divinity manifests itself in the medium of human relationships brought to our attention by a particular method of presentation that both involves and separates us: involves us in its reality, for the 'scenic event that is genuine art is reality' and separates us by its identity as image, 'withdrawn from and inaccessible to us.' We are moved and convinced by this 'polarity' because it corresponds to our characteristic human way of coming into relation with the other, the primal gesture of our wholeness as persons. When we say that theatre both 'involves us' and 'takes us out of ourselves' we speak nothing less than the truth, for this is a 'polar unity', one which focuses our divided attention on a single dimension, drawing us towards itself by the tension that it embodies, in which difference, separation, otherness are not simply recognised but treasured as the ground of human and divine love.

In the first chapter we saw that the imaginative gesture we call 'as if' lies at the root of our awareness of being individual selves, distinct from, but in relation to other people. In theatre this psychological understanding is publicly celebrated so that it becomes a corporate experience embodied in a socio-formative event. Theatres, like religious ritual systems, proclaim the social significance of the individual psychological reaction, giving to each personal gesture a transpersonal meaning and force. In theatre and rite, 'as if' becomes the statement of a present social reality, not merely a gesture of loneliness, of the individual's need to escape from existential isolation and alienation and find refuge in some kind of undifferentiated group expression. Neither rite nor play depends on the corporate hysteria in which reason is temporarily dethroned by emotion and the individual's ability to make personal decisions falls victim to the upsurge of powerful but generalised emotion; neither leads to the abdication of the freedom and ability to criticise the actions and reactions of other people. Our senses are stimulated and not lulled; so long as the rules governing theatre and ritual are understood and observed we are made more, not less aware of the realities that confront us. Over-structured hypnotic theatre and magical ritual, which aim to convince by technical expertise instead of persuading by personal testimony, are revealed as mere tricks of the trade, aimed at psychological manipulation. Within these widened horizons our senses are stimulated not lulled to sleep. We perceive more not less clearly, as those who have been set free from the compulsion to conceal our true identity from ourselves as well as others.

To put this in another way: neither theatre nor ritual functions mechanically, causing those involved to be swept along by forces greater and more powerful than themselves, or rendered less than human by the diversion of their own reality for the creation of something else, something with a life of its own – a monster that has no need to take any notice of the individual awareness it has consumed in order to achieve its present vigorous independence and self-confidence. 'As if' is never a simple matter of cause and effect, some kind of manufactured solution to the problem of personal limitation. It is always a personal response to the nature of man's social being. Any kind of organism may be induced to react in ways belonging to its own nature, but only persons may take it upon themselves to behave 'as if', in the authentically human, genuinely imaginative sense of the phrase. Because theatre and ritual present human life in the language of relationship rather than that of mechanistic causality they proclaim the vital importance of 'as if' as the basis of social understanding.

Theatre, in particular, presents 'as if' in such a way that its nature as public reality cannot be overlooked. Suspension of disbelief is revealed as a basic gesture not only of individual understanding but of social awareness. In particular our understanding of 'as if' has progressed from its role in individual self-formation through its imaginative extension into a way of sharing the experience of other people, to its cultural application in media designed to embody human relational truth rather than merely describing or imitating it. 'As if' takes on the identity of a real place and time, as imagination becomes an adventure with real companions instead of a solitary exercise in fantasy. Theatres are not simply a place where relationship is at work; they are the realisation of the human experience of otherness in its most tangible, most productive form.

There is very much more to theatre than simply the space in which it happens. Space is opportunity, location, the ground for human encounter; as distance, it is the catalyst for relationships between persons. However, it is the frame of human action rather than the action itself, the way that meaning is organised rather than the raw material of life out of which it is constructed. The life of theatre is nothing less than the life of actors and audience, the living presence of real men and women, not simply the presentation of arguments and ideas. It is people we feel rather than emotions; our 'as if' is founded on the recognition of men and women with whom we come into physical contact. Their bodies may be at a distance from our own, but they are people's bodies all the same, identical in kind to those that jostle us in the street or heave up against us in the underground trains. We are aware of them at a level that precedes argument; they are what life is about even before the question has been raised; without even thinking about being interested in them and what happens to them. The flesh we recognise before us on the stage or in the arena is our own flesh, our own reality. Before we get round to imagining ourselves, we recognise ourselves.

This, then, is the underlying circumstance that gives life to theatre, the instinctive 'belief' that precedes the suspension of disbelief. Without this recognition of our own species there would be neither belief nor disbelief. At the level of entertainment (the level of study is not the same) we are only concerned with creatures whom we can conceive to be in some way like ourselves, or whose difference from us seems significant in our own terms – creatures that, one way or another, positively or negatively, illuminate our own condition. The stage is illuminated by just such beings; it is primarily this, rather than the stage lighting, which brings it to life for us, permitting imagination to use aesthetic distance in the way we have described.

In order to fill out this fundamental biological identity there must be the kind of behaviour that we recognise in ourselves. The beings in the stage or arena must be seen to interact in recognisable ways: their joys and sorrows, victories and defeats, loves and hates – and all stages in between – must be like ours. The things that happen to them which either cause or are caused by these reactions must be identifiable as the kinds of things that could happen to us in circumstances that one way or another bear some kind of resemblance to those in the play. A vital theatrical factor in our self-recognition is the organisation of events into patterns whose purpose is to make clear what it is that the author or director regards as the meaning of the actions she or he is presenting. The plot of a play is a special selection of historical or fictional events arranged not strictly chronologically but with regard to the way they relate to one another to bring home the point of the story which is being acted. Strangely enough this kind of editing makes fiction more rather than less realistic, *because it is precisely the way we present ourselves to ourselves*, with more regard to the sense we can make out of the things that happen to us than to the precise order in which they occurred.

Stories are used to present human life as it is, or can be, understood. To this extent they are paradigmatic of human self-accounting. A play's plot, therefore, is one of the principal formulations of its authenticity as human truth; not any particular plot but the fact that it has one. We re-experience our own kinds of sense in the sense-making skill of the playwright, director and actor. This is why Aristotle referred to the plot as 'the soul of the drama' (Butcher, 1951). It is the plot that gives life to the characters rather than the other way round. The plot furnishes those involved with a recognisable life situation; and we recognise the characters as people by the way they react to the circumstances in which they find themselves. Broadly speaking, it is the plot that creates 'as if' by giving rise to the kind of reaction we call empathetic. As for ourselves, we are caught up in the story 'as if' it were our own because at some level we are reminded of our own stories. This is an exceedingly powerful process of association, one which amounts to a kind of psychological assimilation.

This is because of the centrality to our self-understanding of the story itself. We construe the meaning of lives in terms of story. To become a self is to appropriate a past. Stephen Crites puts it like this: 'The first type of unhappiness consists in the failure to appropriate my personal past by making a connected, coherent story of it' (1986, 171).[1] Human understanding itself, says Ernest Keen (in Sarbin, 1986, 187), is the narrative organisation of experience: 'Understanding stories is how human beings understand one another' – a remark that Freud would surely have appreciated. Within the

---

1   Jaques Derrida points out that human being is historic *in itself*, 'That this thought (of Being) is never identical, means first that Being is history' 1978, 147.

dramatological model of human truth the irreducible human datum is not man and man, but story and story. In drama of any kind our stories meet and interpenetrate, prior to drawing apart never to be quite the same again.

Those who stress theatre's didactic effects emphasise the way in which it enlarges our horizons, causing us to accommodate new information within our personal world-view or construct system. No doubt we do this; but much more basic than this, more fundamentally theatrical, is the way in which we read *our* story into that of the *play*, thus contributing to the authenticity of both as expressions of humanity. Given the chance to focus in this way, we lend our eyes to the character so that we see with his or her eyes – and not only our eyes; our hearts, minds and imaginations as well. Again, it is our imagination, our ability to perceive in a way that reflects but does not actually participate in sensory awareness, that allows this to happen; we feel we know what it is like to be this other person. So far as actual teaching goes, it is we who have taught them to be us. It would be closer to the truth to say that our imagination, and that of actor, playwright, director, designer and everyone else involved in the event, empowers them to be both them and us. What we recognise first of all, however, is a congruence of stories which has achieved real flesh before our eyes. Thus our isolation is overcome, and our perception possesses the authority of a corporate statement.

As Aristotle points out, this is first and foremost an emotional event. He has strong views about theatre and its relationship to life, and his opinions are of central importance to the argument of this book. It is not only his view of theatre which concerns us here; we have been influenced, too, by his doctrine of the meaning of life. Classical Greek thought, from which so much of our Western philosophical tradition derives, was dominated by two kinds of approach, two explanations of the world and of life – Plato's and Aristotle's. To put it as succinctly as possible, Plato's view, as expressed in the *Republic*, was that pure Being, final essential reality, could only be found in the world of ideas, because sensory perception, the things and people who's presence we experience, are the images of a celestial archetype, a reality which lies totally outside our field of activities. Human beings exist in the sphere of becoming as opposed to being. For Plato, the Ideal, which is the sphere in which ideas originate, lies not only beyond the human mind, but outside everything else as well. It is the realm of truth, and apart from it there can only be opinion. Only the soul is able to mediate between ideas and appearances. The truth we know and are is only an image of *real* truth, just as (to use his most famous example) the shadow cast on the wall of a cave proclaims the presence of the sun but is not to be confused with its original. The shadow demonstrates our existence, certainly; but it can only be seen because the sun is outside and not inside the cave. Thus the things we perceive both reveal the truth and conceal it; they are images which stand for the Idea while asserting their own difference from it (Russell 1961, 140–1).

Art, however, is even more different from the idea. If, says Plato, life is a reflection of truth, art is a reflection of life. The actual world – earth, plants, animals, mankind – stands nearer to the idea than any imitation of itself (the world that is) could ever do. The artistic imitation of life – *mimesis* – cannot be anything but a dangerous distraction from the truth. "It is conversant with the outward shows and semblances of things, and produce its effect by illusions of form and colour which dupe the senses" (Butcher 1951, 159).

This is very different from Aristotle's philosophy, however. For him, the highest human aim is to become something, for life is essentially an unfolding, a movement from unknowing into the fullness of truth. Minds and bodies and the world that embraces them are actualities, not simply appearances. Indeed they are reality itself – reality in the process of becoming more and more real. For Aristotle the things of this world are not *phainomenoi*, mere perceptions, but *noumenoi*, things that are learned and realised; they are the bearers of truth and meaning, and works of art are their phainomenoi, the means by which their meaning and truth are perceived. Just as for Plato life itself is a metaphor for ultimate meaning, for Aristotle art is a metaphor for life, which is itself ultimate, or bears within itself the seeds of ultimacy.

The most striking example of this is the drama, which is the embodiment of our aspiration towards greater awareness, and consequently more pro-found truth. Its action is revealed in the experience of *catharsis*, our reaction to tragic happenings on stage: "Tragedy is an imitation of an action that is serious, complete and of a certain magnitude; in the form of action not narrative..... through pity and fear, effecting the proper purgation" (Poetics vi, 2, in Butcher, 1951, 249). The portrayal of life in such a way as to reveal the significance of human destiny, says Aristotle, directly alters the quality of the emotions felt by the audience, so that they are somehow purified or 'purged'. In other words, catharsis is the change that takes place in us when art, particularly dramatic art, unlocks humanity, radically affecting the ways in which we feel about one another. It is the experience of healing transfor-mation.

The importance of Aristotle's teaching for any serious consideration of the part played by drama in human life is obvious. Certainly it is central to the argument of this book, and we must spend some time considering it. At first sight it seems a strange doctrine; not, perhaps, with regard to its overall message, that dramatic art is able to put us in touch with profound realities about ourselves and the meaning of our lives; more because of the details it supplies as to how this actually happens. Psychologically speaking, however, it is the way in which it is done that turns out to be most revealing. This is emotional learning, emotional becoming – empathy, understanding with the heart. The emotions distinguished by Aristotle are *pity* and *fear* – pity for *them*, the stage personage or personages in the situation in which they find themselves (and in which we and they find us and them) and fear for *us* who draw ourselves, and are ourselves drawn into, the problem-beset situation that now involves us all: 'Pity and fear, artificially stirred, expel the latent pity and fear which we bring with us from real life, or at least such elements in them as are disquieting, (for) the regulated indulgence of the feelings serves to maintain the balance of nature' (Butcher, 1951, 254).

Aristotle does not consider artistic imitation unreal. It cannot be, because the emotions to which it gives rise, in which it involves spectator and actor alike, are real emotions aroused by something greater, more profound than any ordinary reality can be. It is only through art that we are able to draw near to the real in its ultimate manifestation: 'The work of art is not a semblance opposed to a reality, but the image of a reality which is penetrated by the idea, and through which the idea shows more apparent than in the actual world...the illusions which fine art employs do not cheat the mind; they image forth the immanent idea which cannot find adequate expression under the forms of material existence' (Butcher, 1951, 160, 161). Theatre is emotionally alive: the emotions to which it gives rise mirror the ideal in a way that no other form of communication, or thing communicated, can reproduce. Human emotionality is superior to other dimensions of human awareness, because it is the medium of personal encounter. It is this that brings it into relationship with the ideal, as it were 'over the head' of the real: 'The spectator is lifted out of himself. He becomes one with the tragic sufferer and through him with humanity at large. What is purely personal and self-regarding drops away.' This is particularly true of our identification with heroic figures in plays: 'The spectator who is brought face to face with grander suffering than his own experiences a sympathetic ecstasy, a lifting out of himself' (Butcher, 1951, 267). Here again we have the notion that distance and involvement are interdependent within the theatrical event.

According to Aristotle, theatre depends not simply on arousing emotions which the spectator shares with the stage person into whose story he is imaginatively drawn, but in the way in which these emotions become the vehicle of ideal truth as a result of being purged or purified. In a very famous passage he describes how 'Pity and fear are purged of the impure element which clings to them in life, and in the glow of tragic excitement the feelings are transformed, so that the net result is a noble and emotional satisfaction' (Butcher, 1951, 267). Fontenelle, writing in the eighteenth century, complained that he could not possibly see 'how the emotions can purge the emotions' (in Lucas, 1928, 34n); and yet, according to Aristotle this is precisely what they do. Emotion that is aroused on someone else's part may be too firmly rooted in one's own personal history to be completely altruistic, but the action of relieving our own pain by freely involving oneself in another person's suffering, so that for a short time we are suffering on behalf of someone else transforms the real identity of passions that are customarily expended upon the self and turned away from the other.

This, then, is what Aristotle means when he refers to *catharsis*. Emotion that is purged by encounter promotes encounter. Theatre is able to set the healing and transforming process going by arranging the circumstances of aesthetic distance. Pain is expelled when egoism is redirected; this in itself involves powerful feelings. Pity for the other transforms fear that one may be – indeed is – involved in his or her pain; fear is taken up into pity and redeemed by it, as our way of perceiving life is purified by the intensity of our involvement in the story-world of the play. This is the phenomenon that we call 'aesthetic distance' in which disbelief itself lays the foundation for a poetic transformation of human feeling from selfishness to love.

Again we see the true nature of theatre as a truthful trick. The artifice lies not in importing something new into what we might call 'natural' human truth about relationship, certainly not in fabricating a kind of creation, theatrical relationship, which will stand on its own, having been put together in a certain way to do a particular kind of job, that of making up the differences in ordinary human encounter. Theatre explores, it does not create – and in exploring it enables and empowers. The microscope does not invent the world it reveals; on the contrary, its mechanical tool-like nature is swallowed up in the independent reality to which it draws our attention. I have written elsewhere that 'Both comedy and tragedy originated in our perception of the relationship between subject and object as something which cannot be divided: it is always 'me' and 'not me' at the same time. The movement of recoil by which we withdraw to a safe distance in order to contemplate someone else's predicament without becoming involved always seems an inadequate kind of defence. The more we try to keep aloof, the more we are involved' (Grainger, 1985, 93).

After all, involvement is our real purpose. The way in which we suffer and rejoice with and in one another is our field of exploration. The experience of catharsis only takes place where there is an intention of self-giving, a sympathetic impulse of encounter and involvement directed towards another person. The use of the artistic medium of the stage personage, the dramatic character, serves to direct and intensify this impulse and to provide a meeting-place for spectator and artist. This cathartic art, the art of staged meetings and artificially induced encounters, promotes relationship because it is an artificial arrangement of ideas and things which expresses and embodies our human need to give and receive, ceaselessly to rediscover our own true being in an exchange of life.

We have said that catharsis is an emotional rather than an intellectual phenomenon; that it is, as Aristotle claims, a discharge of feelings which succeeds in changing the nature of an existing feeling-state, freeing it from elements that disturb and distort it. At the same time, it depends on the understanding which triggers such a response and gives rise to a release of feelings that itself brings intellectual clarity as both thought and feeling are captured in a single image. In catharsis ideas and emotions take flight at the same time, each contributing to the force of the other, and intellectual judgements are forged in the heat of a powerful affective response. This is because catharsis is a function of the clarity of a perceptual image exercising a degree of attraction which is enough to lead those who are exposed to it to allow themselves to be drawn into its sphere of influence, with results that are highly emotional. The least willingness to collaborate with the forces exerted by the image brings about the experience of immersion in the feelings it projects. As we have seen, this willingness to co-operate with the image's action is directly connected with an assurance of safety and security associated with emotional distance from the events portrayed.

At this point, we may return to Bertolt Brecht and his celebrated *verfremdungseffekt* or 'alienation effect' which stressed the theatrical nature of stage performances by continually shattering the illusion of real life. Brecht's theatre aims at *controlled* involvement leading to more balanced judgement. It would be a mistake to suppose his aim was simple detachment, the critical as opposed to the involved point of view. What in fact he had in mind was real engagement with the problems confronting his characters. He used theatricality in order to render ideas, objects, situations – and people – *unlike* life, permitting them to stand out in relief, their meaning dictated by their own logic, having broken away from the network of assumptions and expectations which enmeshes them in ordinary life. The world presented in this way can speak for itself *as* itself, rather than simply as what we have always assumed it to be, this is what Shelley meant when he said that "Poetry makes familiar objects to be as if they were not familiar". The ability of theatre to isolate and intensify images was to be used to give clarity to meaning by making us really appreciate things we had begun to take for granted. By breaking the illusion he rendered the spectator/participant's grasp on the emotional reality of the dramatic situation problematic enough to require a more conscious kind of involvement, a greater determination to come to grips with a *truth more real than its theatrical image was seductive*, an emotional and intellectual reality underpinning the circumstances involved in a fictional presentation. By demonstrating that fiction was fiction, Brecht made his audience more determined to own the facts to which fiction pointed, so that what was to be learned from allowing oneself to become involved in the story constituted a real investment in life rather than simply a refreshing journey into make-believe. Unless the truth behind the fiction could some-how be separated from the plausible presentation of fiction as fact, and identification became a conscious intention rather than an automatic re-sponse, the truth would vanish with the fiction that sustained it, and insight be left behind with cigarette stubs and discarded theatre tickets.

   The research of a generation of semioticists – students of signs as carriers of meaning – gives support to this notion that real identification thrives on its own interruption. At the level of putting plays together our imagination is engaged in a process of decodifying a narrative in order to re-assemble its various parts into a sequence which permits the highest level of surprise and uncertainty, the greatest opportunity for stressing the difference between the world of the play and that of the audience by withholding knowledge which is essential to the understanding of those confined in one sphere or the other. The re-arrangement of narrative into plot aims always at the maximisation of opportunity for dramatic irony; someone, somewhere, is always being kept by the structure of the play in a state of public ignorance and private confusion. A process of 'defamiliarisation' runs counter to the purpose of letting us in on what is happening. Time and again, by one dramatic technique or another, the medium itself proclaims to us that it is not 'like life' while continuing, by its very willingness to rearrange and distort the evidence, to play upon the fact that we continue to recognise our own lives in it. By rewriting its stories in order to maximise their potential for confusion and conflict, drama provides us with an opportunity to indulge in the struggle for personal meanings which is the very nature of human psychology.

   Indeed, some modern playwrights have concentrated their efforts on encouraging a kind of paradoxical identification to take place. In the way that drama questions its own methods, its own identity, we are able to recognise our own experience of self-hood:

   'A play which requires the spectators to 're-examine the rules' of
   drama demands his/her collaboration and active participation in the

production of meaning. Such a re-examination challenges the spectator's relation to both the dramatic world and the actual world.' (Aston and Savona, 1991, 33)

Aston and Savona see contemporary theatre audiences as 'positioned by the conjunction of 'radical' text and anti-illusionistic performance aesthetic, at a critical remove from the dramatic fiction' (1991, 46).

All of this supports our contention about the relation of *distance*, by which we mean every kind of reason, from our own common sense to the playwright's explicit instructions, to resist becoming involved in the play – and *catharsis*, which is the result of ignoring all this and allowing the action of the play to affect our own feelings about ourselves by a process of identification with its characters. We believe that there is no contradiction, and that, in fact, distance is instrumental in bringing about catharsis. The evidence seems to suggest, however, that there is nothing automatic or inevitable about this. Semiotic investigation leads to the conclusion that in order to result in catharsis, emotional involvement, identification of a character's situations with my own, ought not to come too easily if that character is to have any chance of carrying me with him on his journey towards meaning. There would seem to be an optimal distance necessary for theatre to achieve the kind of psychological significance that gives rise to real 'changes of mind'. Imagination, having once been aroused by the theatrical mode of presenting its evidence about life (dependent on one hand on an artificial intensified perceptual image, and on the other, with the audience's stated intention to use their imaginations) must be regulated and controlled in order to achieve catharsis, which occurs at the point where the framework of theatrical technique is abandoned and yet the play survives. At this point, when we can no longer in any way fictionalise our feelings but must come face to face with our ownership of them, our involvement with the play's meaning reaches a climax and we find release in allowing ourselves to be ourselves in a new way, as people who have succeeded in becoming aware of their own vulnerability, the wounded nature which is their personal truth, acknowledgement of which constitutes their sole claim to authenticity.

Catharsis, then, is the crisis brought about by our recognition of what is fictional in ourselves and our world. Because it is able to use its own fictions to establish genuine human truth theatre provides us with evidence that truth is stronger than fiction. The processes that give rise to catharsis are closer to the problem-solving, 'grit in the oyster', model of human cognition than some have supposed. Certainly it seems to take place at the limits of our power to remain aloof, when the effort to keep at a safe distance from what is happening to us finally collapses, and we find ourselves personally involved in a reality that disturbs but cannot destroy us. Our new found ability to survive the emotional turmoil we feared does not consist in having 'seen through' the play and dismissed it as fiction without any relevance to ourselves; indeed it is the discovery of its emotional significance that moves us so much. The safety of make-believe leads us into the dangerous presence of truths about ourselves which are still with us when we come to our senses, and find that a play about masks has succeeded in reminding us of our own.

For Thomas Scheff (1979), aesthetic distance is not a general term referring to the juxtaposition of spectator and play (or other work of art), but a specific point of balance between involvement and separation at which catharsis occurs, which is expressed and embodied in the presentation of art. Catharsis happens when we are secure enough in our defensive spectator-hood to allow ourselves to take chances, not with our truth but with our manipulation of it. The skill of theatre lies in bringing us to this point by means of the creation and destruction of a social convention that assures us of our emotional non-involvement.

All this suggests that aesthetic distance refers to a particular degree of psychological threat rather than serving as a generalised description of a state of affairs in which audiences are kept geographically separate from actors by the setting aside of a privileged area for the construction of a new dramatic world. Distance is not only as space to be filled, but a point on a scale, a degree of engagement. Scheff (1979) describes the state of affairs resulting in a cathartic response in terms of a balance between safety and danger corresponding to the degree of attraction and repulsion felt towards an imagined situation projected by a theatrical image. According to the intensity of the image and their own degree of psychological defensiveness, individuals differ in their willingness to allow themselves to imagine that what is presented before them is actually happening to them, and to feel the emotions that would naturally arise in them if such were the case. Like Freud and Bruner, Scheff locates the therapy of catharsis in the opportunity it provides for those involved to re-live occasions in their own personal histories when they were unable to allow themselves to react emotionally in the right way; in a way, that is, which would have brought them face-to-face with the reality of what was happening to them, so they could work through their trauma instead of forcing it to find its own ways of asserting its importance at the cost of their peace of mind in the future.

Catharsis occurs, says Scheff, when individuals feel safe enough to allow the play to remind them of things they have succeeded in forgetting, but really need to remember and re-live. Theatre provides a distanced encounter with feelings that require acknowledgement and incorporation within consciousness. If people are 'optimally distanced' – that is, protected and exposed at the same time – they will drop their well-established psychological defences and open themselves up to emotions they have longed to feel and been too frightened to allow themselves to remember. People in this position are conscious of being secure enough to 'see themselves feeling'. They can encounter the feelings which terrify and appal them while witnessing their ability to survive them. Danger has not been negated or denied – far from it, for the imagery of anger and fear is presented as powerfully as it can be, in order that its defeat may be all the more salutary. It has simply been exorcised by a more potent reality, that of aesthetic distance, in which the spectator is reassured and established by the ability to distinguish between what the image *says* and what in fact it *is* and to take account of both realities, drawing strength from the latter while finding release in the former. In theatre we witness ourselves triumphing over our own fear, the 'double vision' which brings catharsis, our long overdue absolution from the effect of unacknowledged feelings. Thus, the same theatrical image protects and exposes in order to mediate the cathartic response, which owes its universality to the fact that at some time in their lives, usually during their earliest years, human beings have been subjected to feelings of a kind and an intensity as to render them incapable of being retained within the conscious mind, and have sought relief through catharsis.

> 'The child draws into himself to feel the pain, puts his head down and cries, but frequently looks at his mother to see if the situation is still safe. While feeling the pain, the child also sees himself through the mother's eyes...' (Scheff, 1979, 62).

Being allowed to cry helps children to adjust to the losses which 'appear to be an inescapable feature of infancy as a result of intense and incommunicable feelings of separation and loss' (Scheff, 1979, 54 n.1). On the other hand, grief that is not worked through in the genuine discharge of feeling stands in the way of future attachments because of the danger of future loss. Scheff claims that theatre and ritual militate against emotional repression to produce personal relationship and group solidarity. 'The feelings of relief from tension, increased clarity of thought and perception and heightened fellow feeling which follow collective catharsis give rise to powerful forces of cohesion and group solidarity' (1979, 53).

Whether catharsis is collective or individual, it is always a matter of a balance of danger and safety. It is only at the balance point that feelings are both near enough to the surface of consciousness to demand expression, and sufficiently distanced from consciousness to allow the relaxation of psychological defences: 'At aesthetic distance there is...deep emotional resonance, but also a feeling of control. If a repressed emotion...is re-stimulated at aesthetic distance, the crying that results is not unpleasant... the person feels refreshed when it is over.' (1979, 64) Scheff speaks of refreshment rather than emotional purging, but both he and Aristotle associate the same kind of psychological reaction with the appropriate staging of works of dramatic art.

The balance between structure and freedom, safety and danger on which catharsis depends is illustrated by the shape of theatres but does not only function in theatrical surroundings. Theatre presents it most dramatically. This does not mean it was first presented in this way, however. As Alida Gersie and Nancy King point out, the same principle governs catharsis in storytelling. 'The outer eye may register a familiar room or people – but the inner eye generates images of less familiar worlds and beings.' We need to surrender to the unknown of the tale, for 'We are about to travel from one kind of known world to the next which is unknown; we may not like it at all. Here again, our fear is of encounter with the unknown and unassimilated Other.' Gersie and King describe how 'the storyteller becomes the guide through the unknown realms. Although we need to surrender to the unknown of the tale, we can only do so if we trust that our guide knows the way' (1990, 33). In storytelling, the element of safety consists largely in the trust developed by the teller: 'The relationship between teller and listener is always intimate. The closeness is generated by the interconnection between the one who tells and the one who listens' (1990, 32) – but this interconnection is a sharing in the same symbolic structure. Here again, catharsis depends on a shared understanding. A story is a story, just as a play is a play. The reassurance given by the theatrical setting is provided in story-telling by circumstances – a setting – indissolubly linked with story: 'Two people sitting near one another. One is telling a story, the other is listening. In the space between storyteller and listener images will arise.' In fact the images create the space. They give room for an encounter of persons. The between-ness of story, like theatrical distance, is without actual dimensions. It takes place wherever people feel safe enough to face the danger of putting themselves in the place imagination has cleared for them – whether this be in a play, in a story, in a theatre, or by a fire-side. Just as in theatres there is some kind of signal that things are about to begin, the world of the play is about to be born, so stories are announced in unmistakeable ways. Instead of the raising of a curtain and the dimming of house lights, there is a book taken up in a particular way, a request for people to make themselves specially comfortable; perhaps a pair of reading glasses adjusted, the dimming and focussing of lamps to provide 'atmosphere'. Certainly, almost inevitably, there are words associated in one form or another with storytelling the world over: 'When we listen to a 'Once upon a time…' tale, listeners are allowed to identify to their heart's content' (Gersie and King, 1990, 38).

In stories, as in plays, we identify willingly with people we imagine to be in danger, or suffering pain or distress, or undergoing violent emotion, because we know that the circumstances are fictional. In theatre the willingness comes from our awareness that this is a play. In storytelling it comes from our knowledge that this is a story. Plays are signalled as plays by their theatrical setting, consisting of an acting area, physically separated from an auditorium, by the presence of people acting as if they are the people in the play, by special scenery, lighting, sound effects, etc. Stories are announced to be stories by the narrative framework of a verbal kind: ('Once upon a time…'). Both plays and stories are characterised by belief in the imaginative world they create – a belief they require from others and possess themselves. In a way imagination must work harder on stories than plays because of the actual presence of living characters. However, the harder our imagination works, the more of ourselves we invest in the effort to pretend we are living in the same world as the personages in the story, and the more real and satisfactory our experience turns out to be.

This last is a very important point. It is our willingness to invest ourselves in the experience which makes it vivid and emotionally satisfying. Our willingness, however, depends on our ability to let ourselves take this step into the unknown. Catharsis, the healing release of self towards another, is always a kind of negotiation between opposing forces. The greater the involvement required in order to make the story 'live', the stronger and more trustworthy the protective framework must be. In order to encourage people to 'forget' their surroundings and lose themselves in a story, you must spend time in making them feel very comfortable indeed! In fact, it is the intimacy of a story that encourages us to open ourselves to experiencing the vulnerability of others – 'You asked for a story, and now I've told you one. Not too long and not too short. Just the distance between you and me…' (Gersie and King, 1990, 41). Seen in this light, theatre is a way of making intimacy more widely available.

CHAPTER 6

Image and Archetype

Aristotle and Artaud

Aristotle's definition of theatrical catharsis has not gone unquestioned. According to Thomas Scheff, it is 'probably the most controversial sentence ever written'. The principal objection has always been the one directed against any kind of explanation of human phenomena which sees feeling rather than thought as the main explanatory factor. As Scheff says, 'Emotions play very little part in theories of social behaviour. They are either omitted entirely or, at best, treated as an undifferentiated residue' (1979, 3). However, Aristotle is very much concerned with actual artistic experience rather than with explanations of the artistic process. The celebrated nineteenth century critic S.H. Butcher comments that in his actual treatment of particular arts such as poetry and music, 'He assumes a subjective end, consisting in a certain pleasurable emotion, although his general theory of aesthetics regards the overall purpose of art to be the purely objective one of realising the εἶδος in concrete form' (1951, 209).

Aristotle's critics have not forgiven him for his 'descent' into phenomenology. D.D. Raphael claims that it originates in desire to counter Plato's view that dramatic art merely encourages self-pity instead of endurance, as we find ourselves sympathising with the struggles of the protagonists. Instead, according to Aristotle, 'We blow off steam and so are purged,' which he considers to be an unworthy response to other people's pain (1960, 15). Similarly, F.L. Lucas reminds us that 'The theatre is not a hospital' (1928, 29). Both Raphael and Lucas prefer a more intellectual doctrine of tragedy, Lucas attributing its fascination to the power of curiosity, 'The first intellectual emotion of the child and the last of the old man' (1928, 52) and Raphael to a sense of human sublimity: 'Vis à vis the audience, the spiritual grandeur of the hero is balanced by their god-like omniscience' (1960, 31). Raphael is particularly unimpressed by ideas about emotional involvement and transformed feelings, adopting a straightforward view of aesthetic distance as a simple protective mechanism against involvement: 'Classical and romantic tragedians alike place their characters at a distance of time, place and status in order to produce an impersonal contemplation'. The possibility that there may be more to the theatrical event than rational conclusions drawn from the direct statements it makes about life is not entertained for a moment, a fact that is itself dramatically revealed by the following comment on Sophocles' *Theban Plays*: 'No member of Sophocles' audience was likely to suppose himself in any danger of murdering his father and marrying his mother' (1960, 16). Well – not consciously , perhaps. Not everything that happens in theatres is entirely conscious, however.

The power of theatrical catharsis is a hidden force. We are set at a distance and left to draw our own conclusions. Or so it seems. In fact we are distanced in order to become involved, thought being drawn into action in order to be transformed by feeling. It is not possible to think of emotions and intellect separately here. To divide them, giving more significance to one that the other, is to remove any possibility of understanding. As in life, so in art, understanding and feeling are mutually dependent. Theatre forces us to take the psycho-genitive world-changing force of emotion with the kind of seriousness it deserves in every sphere of life, but rarely receives. The theatrical image stands out as thought-through-feeling, feeling-through-thought, greeting us as spectators and, before we know what is happening, transforming us into participants in a new reality, in which cognition and affect rediscover each other and we are confirmed as persons. So intense is this relationship of idea and experience within the theatrical image that it stands out as a unique presence in our social awareness, as if to intensify experience to such a degree as to give it the power to reproduce itself in those whom it encounters, or at least to make latent things salient and operative – a crystallisation of life which is able to work as a catalyst to restore balance in the place of emotional and intellectual distortion.

In its origin catharsis depends on the image-making faculty of the psyche. In particular it is associated with the process of identification whereby we are imaginatively united with someone who is not ourself but henceforward belongs to our sense of self. The kind of identification involved in theatrical catharsis is 'secondary' rather than 'primary'. In other words it is identification *with regard to* someone else rather than simply *with* them. In infancy, primary identification means that the infant takes its mother into itself, the entire maternal environment contributing to a single uniting awareness. Secondary identification, however, is a genuinely social experience, and emerges when the growing child identifies the presence and rights of others as distinct from itself. The movement is not one of simple expansion by extending the boundaries of the self, but an alliance entered into with someone who is clearly defined, experientially known, as *not* the self. The satisfaction associated with this kind of fully personal identification is experienced in terms of movement away from the self towards the imagined other; he or she imagined as other and not merely part of oneself. This is to be the substance of our most personal joys for the rest of our lives.

The meaning of the image that is interiorised is independence of the self rather than subservience to it. Obviously it is our image in the sense that we entertain its presence 'in our mind's eye'. It is the way in which we lay hold on a reality originating outside ourselves which we wish to bring into close relationship with us. Images exist within their own psychic space, pointing away from the self as a perceiving subject towards the other as a source of meaning and value with which we wish to be associated but not to control. Archetypal psychology, as developed by James Hillman, regards this imaginal space between two people as 'the sense of soul, the middle ground of psychic realities.' Images 'are the psyche itself in its imaginative visibility' (1988, 4, 5, 7, 23). As shadow gives substance, revealing depth beyond and between, the soul-psyche underlines our active embodied presence in the world. This is the image as focus of relationship. It is not to be confused with the world of private fantasy – or indeed with anything else that is reducible to the mind's self-reflected activity. Image is primary datum: not what one sees, but the means by which one sees. Jung (1953) refers to it as 'a psychological activity of creative nature'. Thus, an image of ourselves in relation to someone else is not the way in which we present our own experience to ourselves, but the way that soul – the poetic awareness of meanings beyond meanings – presents itself to *us*.[1] If this is true of all natural phenomena, as Hillman claims, it must be particularly the case with regard to the image that we receive of other people. Theatrical experience demonstrates that, whatever Freud may say, image gives rise to emotion. Armstrong (1971) speaks of an 'affecting presence', one which invites our involvement in an emotional relationship. This, of course, is the *sine qua non* of cathartic identification.

In fact, our experience is completely the opposite of any sense of control which we impose upon the image with which we identify; it is the image that directs *us*, reflecting ourselves back on ourselves as we compare ourselves with it in the attempt to mould ourselves to its outcome. It is as if the internalised image were the source of a personal message from someone

---

1   In neo-Platonic thought, 'soul' could signify both my own and the world's soul.

whom we know very intimately, and are eager not to offend or put off in any way. Indeed, the image is experienced as inalienably personal, personal in *itself*, not simply because it belongs to us.

In what sense does it belong to us? We did not invent it, or take it over. We simply welcomed it into our awareness in its identity as itself, treasuring it for its qualities of being unlike us and hoping that the qualities and functions of the person it represents to us will somehow become transferred onto us rather than the other way round. The identified image of another person is much more than an idea we have about them; it is the symbol of their presence and influence within our lives. Thus, the images of living and dying that make up our works of art are themselves the reflections of an internalised other. Our individual universes are held together by such messages, which we regard as the foundation for our attempts to structure our own experience in ways that will reveal the meaning implicit in it – a meaning that comes from, and refers to, what is not ourselves but the reflection of a truth beyond our grasp, the sameness and difference we call relationship. The image of another person with which we identify retains its ability to keep us and them in relationship because it is quite specifically *the image of otherness* not sameness, giving rise to a sense of ourselves in someone else's regard, enabling us to see through their eyes and so become like them.

Thus the image with which we identify is not simply an idea that we have about somebody else, but a relationship that we sustain and in which we abide. The satisfaction given by this kind of social identification comes from sharing across boundaries of selfhood, the giving and receiving of being. We do not take the other over and include them in ourselves, but receive them as an image presented to us which, because it is an image of personhood, may be entertained in our awareness as a life-giving stranger. This is how it is with all our highest level constructs, each of which has authority over the way we look at life, each of which is essentially personal (Durkheim and Mauss, 1963, 82).

In the theatre the phenomenon we have called 'as if' is not an idea but a living image. As such it cannot be grasped and assimilated, but only reached out to and met. Such an encounter meets our personal needs in a way that no theoretical understanding ever could, for this is in fact how we really know one another – not by familiarising ourselves with the principles and conditions of their existence but by being received into their embodied presence, either in actual or imagined social conditions. Theatre combines both these options.

This use of the word 'image' to mean the presence of the other person is a metaphor taken from perceptual process, the specific process of visual discrimination that theatre is designed to intensify. The action of focusing perception renders the perceived object fascinating to us; we find ourselves drawn into the image which is rendered free of distractions; the person or object we are attending to is the only occupant of its universe and the only example of its particular kind. As such it presents to us as all such persons or objects, the inescapable symbol of its own being. Thus a chair or a table alone in a space illuminated under theatrical conditions stands in for the idea of chair- or table-ness revealed in concrete form. The ability of the image, external or internal, to be significant in and for itself renders it attractive to us as the source of poetic meaning, draws us into relationship with it. Its ability to direct us to the 'soul of things' gives it a powerful emotional impact. This '*deictic*' (Elam, 1988, 22) quality of objects, including people, who are presented as parts of a play comes from their identity as focused images. 'Staging' of this kind has the effect of 'releasing events from their literal understanding into a mythical appreciation' (Hillman, 1983b, 27), liberating us from the reductionist oppositions of 'fact' versus 'fiction', life-giving subject versus lifeless object, science versus wishful thinking, that impoverish our experience of human-ness.

In art we are presented with a special kind of phenomenon which speaks the language of life without being life-like – without deceiving us with regard to its true identity. Presented life is not really like life as we experience it, life 'in the raw'. We are under no real illusions about this. The image is a focusing of meanings drawn from life, expressed in human speech, move-ment, gesture, etc.; but it is not actually that life in the form in which we characteristically experience it, nor does it pretend to be. Indeed the dis-claimer is an integral, formative part of its message. As a work of art the stage event draws attention to its own nature as something presented, directed, wholly intentional, not to be overlooked. Something outstanding, in fact. Thus, the message to be proclaimed is the same thing as the message about how this is being done. Both occupy what has been called 'deictic space', or space which points to itself, and which it contains. In the act of *foregrounding* (to use Goffman's phrase) the play draws attention to its own special way of working as well as to the importance of the events it presents. This is not surprising, as foregrounding is essentially demonstrable, and cannot avoid being recognised as such. It is what *all* plays are about, whatever stage convention is adopted. Even the most naturalistic playing and direction, because of the medium it uses to express itself, will always be self-referential.

One of the main, if not *the* main functions of theatre is the objectification of the image. This fact should be established early on in any examination of the healing nature of theatrical experience, simply because of the pathological implications of various ways in which the image of the world may be distorted. Theatre makes us take immediate account of what is not ourself but has the very greatest relevance to ourself: the other experienced and understood precisely as other. The event of theatre provides us with evidence against a literalistic explanation of perception in which we simply accept the evidence of our senses and adjust our experience in accordance with it, and an idealist one which maintains that we ourselves are entirely responsible for what we perceive, our perception of otherness being a straightforward projection of our own self. Theatre makes the other stand out as similar to ourselves and yet fascinatingly different. At the most fundamental level, it transforms familiar phenomena by concentrating our attention on their new appearance in a way that we find perceptually distracting – and by the use of colour, sound and movement, sensually attractive. The Roman scientist-philosopher Lucretius describes an experience of focused theatrical pleasure:

> 'When the saffron russet and violet awnings stretched over great theatres, unfurled over masts and cross-beams, flap and undulate, they dye all the scene below, projecting their rippling colours onto the audience packed on the benches, the entire spectacle of the stage and the splendid part occupied by the senators. *The more the theatre is shut in by the surrounding hoardings and the less daylight is admitted, the more the enclosed area laughs in a flood of gaiety.*' [our italics] (Trans. Ferguson Smith 1969, 131)

Thus, in order to prevent itself from appearing as part of our world that we create or control, the theatrical image has to draw us into its own world, so that we may see things in a way that is recognisably distinct from ours, recognisably *its own*.

In doing this, of course, it simply reproduces our characteristic human experience whenever we try to understand the world of other people and things. In order to know anything – or anybody – as itself, we have to acknowledge its separate existence to the extent of actually experiencing it: this is someone or something else, and I want to know about them. In fact, the evidence of things is stronger and more conclusive than that of persons, for as we have seen, we actually make things into persons in order to overcome the difference that exists between us, the difference between the animate and the inanimate: 'To understand anything at all, we must envision it as having an independent subjective interior existence, capable of experience, obliged to a history, motivated by purposes and intentions. We must always think anthropomorphically, even personally' (Hillman, 1972, 16). We remember ideas and events through stories organised around the figures of their central characters. From the beginning of our personal awareness the world is personal, its categories understood by association with the people we recognise. The sense perceptions we have are always and indissoluably the icons of a personal awareness which precedes them and directs their organisation into what we know to be our own individual, even idiosyncratic, view of the world, one that we privately consider to be reasonable primarily *because* it is ours. Recognition of personal meanings governs the mind's organisation; the people who invite us on-stage and into their world are not simply women and men who may be like or unlike ourselves, they are a living image of the ways in which we have constructed our own awareness. Held in focus before us, they have the power to convince and to move.

If Jung was right, this power operates at a deeper level than the consciousness of individual men and women and on a wider scale than that covered by anybody's personal autobiography. James Hillman is concerned to establish psychological awareness as a relationship each of us enter into with an underlying truth of person-hood which is so far from being a mere function of our own individuality as to be the reality that precedes, transcends and undergirds it. The archetypes of the collective unconscious contact the individual awareness through the images of the imagination which we ourselves receive but do not create: 'The egocentric psyche…may grudgingly admit personifying as a figure of speech, but never that the imaginal realm and its persons are actual presences and true powers' (1972, 41). The archetypal original and reference of the personified image, says Hillman, can alone account for its power to lead us into relationships that transform us, feelings of love originating in our perception of the image as personal and irresistible. Indeed, for a love to know what it is loving, it must personify, because as Unamuno says, 'We only love that which is like ourselves' (1969, 131).

Like ourselves, but not part of ourselves. The image comes from elsewhere. We focus on the fantasy presented before us, the image that holds us, the experience that contains us. It is because the experience is given that it can be accepted and lived as itself. All the machinery of theatre, imaginative and technical, physical and psychological, functions 'on behalf of' others, treating the other as if they were the self. All of it is used to assert the difference on which 'as if' depends. The image is received as another person, or an object in which I have invested meaning, an objective illustration or example of my power to uncover meaning outside myself; the play itself asserts its independent identity as a piece of fiction which in performance assumes its own life, separate from author and director as well as from audience. Division between auditorium and stage has its own tangible, geographo-kinetic reality as does that between the brightly lit acting area and the darkness that surrounds it. The theatrical image itself moves into itself, a three-dimensional picture of life that literally moves away from the spectator in order to draw her or him after it into its own world, the deepened image producing involvement – what Hillman refers to as 'the depth dimension of soul now entering the subjective structures of consciousness' (1972, 212). In all these ways, soul is entertained as a visitor for whom we have made the most expensive and careful preparations, about whose arrival we can never be certain. At least we have provided her with a place to be, one which she seems to enjoy; and the play itself, the most immediate and essential embodiment of the image, will provide, in its rediscovery of the timeless themes of human life the kind of language she prefers to use. As Hillman says: 'A mythic manner of speaking is fundamental to the soul's way of formulating itself' (1972, 20).

The personified image represents the psyche in all its forms, an endless succession of fantasied relationships, a role repertoire that can never be catalogued because life consists precisely in its adaptability, its total imaginative freedom. The plays that seize our attention spring to life by the way that the image resounds with our own psychological life, awakening within us the memory of experiences we have never had, carrying us into areas of understanding we believed ourselves too rigidly set in our ways to enter. The play awakens us to possibilities of being that we would not otherwise consider in connection with ourselves, and does so by means of 'An independent primacy of the imaginal that creates its fancies autonomously, ceaselessly, spontaneously' (1972, 100). This notion of the independence of the image is characteristically Jungian: psychological understanding and spiritual insight are the gifts of the shared unconscious to the individual ego, which is why we experience moments of enlightenment and the deepening of awareness over time as truth that is disclosed to us rather than as the product of our own mental processes. The complex *dramatis personae* of our imaginative life bear witness to the scope of our own potential ways of being in the world; the images of fantasy are given us in order to help us walk in as yet unknown places and develop new ways of acting and reacting in the world. The inscape of our personal psyche consists of personified images revealed to us in dreams and traditional stories which are endlessly reproduced in all kinds of works of art, both figurative or representational and abstract, according to the degree to which the image is articulated in narrative form.

If this is so, then the function of theatre is very greatly enhanced. We do not simply recognise people who are like ourselves, people whom we are conscious are playing a role in some way similar to ours, but are made aware of deeper, more stimulating possibilities concerned with those whom we do not consciously resemble at all. Confronted by the fascinating image of the other, we begin to recognise ourselves in the kinds of people whom we have admired or despised but never understood. In Jungian terms, the play brings before us the archetypes that we have ignored or neglected and invites us to enlarge our awareness through our contact with them. In theatre the imaginal life of the shared unconscious is physically expressed and speaks in and through the world of concrete objects and embodied people. The realm of psychodynamics is presented psychodramatically by means of the living, embodied image. The theatre does not invent the process, it merely puts it into practice in a particularly striking and effective way. The images it presents are brought before us during the course of our ordinary social lives every time we allow ourselves to think and feel freely, and to trust the images that arise, following where they lead so that they can contribute to whatever it is that we may have already decided to be or do. Because of its archetypal resonance the theatrical image embodies an endless range of ways of being in the real world which are not mere inventions but identifiable psychic pathways. Insofar as the subject matter of play is expressed in images that are authentically personal, it will speak to us of things we already know about, in the way that it wishes us to know about them. Wise playwrights study these archetypes, precisely because they are universal, and because no amount of hard work or ingenuity will succeed in getting them to alter the song they have always sung.

Theatre, however, renders the song irresistible. The most prosaic piece of theatre is rendered poetic by the business of being staged; the intensified image seizes our attention with the urgency belonging to vital personal communications, urging us to look as closely as we can, to penetrate the surface layer of perception and discover its hidden truth, the significance it must surely have in order to be able to force itself on attention in such a way. Thus the mechanics of theatrical production open us to the existence of metaphor and symbol, tuning us in to events and presences which are already charged with the meta-meaning of religious myth. Archetypal psychology regards ordinary behaviour as if it were part of an extraordinary drama whose plot concerns the underlying significance of human living and dying. The effect of actual stage presentation is to bring such things to the surface by reproducing the dramatic story of the experiences of individuals and nations in circumstances which demonstrate its metaphorical identity and archetypal significance. The artificiality of the theatrical image, its way of depending on our willingness to 'suspend our disbelief' bears additional witness to its nature as a kind of distraction, something to be seen through and not under any circumstances taken literally. The real meaning lies below the surface, at the very heart of the image's impact upon our individual awareness. It is a beckoning absence, the very essence of 'as if'.

Theatre communicates the truth of encounter more effectively than any kind of dogma can possibly do. Instead of taking analogy for granted, as theology and philosophy do so often, thereby running the risk of forgetting it altogether and substituting simple homology, theatre brings home the metaphorical purpose of its procedures. 'As if' is not simply an axiom which possesses explanatory power; indeed it is the very opposite, for it points to the absence of logical connections and does not hesitate to 'move the goalposts' in its search for an answer to the problem. 'Fictions,' says Hillman 'are not supposed to have great explanatory power, so they do not settle things for a mind searching for fixity. But they do provide a resting place for a mind searching for ambiguity and depth... "As if" perspectives...satisfy the aesthetic, religious and speculative imagination more than they do the intellect' (1972, 151). Plays may themselves proceed in ways that are logical and straightforward; but the idea of 'doing a play' and the actual play itself, both text and performance, are leaps of the imagination, voyages into fantasy for the purpose of bringing back another kind of truth – the wholly metaphorical truth of 'as if' which cannot be used as the logical solution of a problem, but only as a way of increasing our enlightenment about life.

This is a more naturalistic approach than might at first appear, since the significance of logic in human affairs always tends to be more theoretical than actual. Psychologists of cognition are almost united in stressing the presence of an imaginative fictional factor in every kind of sense perception and also in our intellectual assessment of situations involving ourselves, particularly those which have personal significance for the way in which we see ourselves. This being so, the imaginative, myth-revealing method of theatre turns out to be a more accurate way of understanding the relational life of men and women than some other approaches of a more scientific or nomothetic kind. Implicitly or explicitly, theatre employs a mythopoeic approach to human reality, one specifically designed for dealing with significances and persons, rather than objects and things. In the mythic themes of theatre, objectivity and subjectivity combine to produce a living symbolism which is the human experience of relationship, that state of being in which self and other meet without becoming confused. Such is my involvement in the play that its action is my own while remaining free of my control and outside the limits of my identity – which after all is my experience of being involved in life itself. There is nothing very logical about that, and yet it is the case.

The actors and actresses presented to us under these conditions draw us into their world to share joys and sorrows, successes and failures, fortunes and misfortunes. How could we do otherwise, who are accustomed to identifying with the image of others? Meanwhile, the performers themselves, if they are aiming at any kind of naturalism, must perpetually be cutting their gestures down to size and restraining their own human urge to be dramatic... It is *this* situation, *these* people we ask you to be concerned with, they say; attend to us as persons not images, do not be so eager to universalise us at the expense of our uniqueness.

The image continues to exert its fascination however, try as we may to keep hold of our freedom of choice in the matter of identification. We find ourselves rejoicing with the joyful and weeping with those who weep; protesting against social injustice done to others, resentful about exploitation we ourselves are not suffering, guilty of offences committed in our absence and without our consent. We have done these things and felt these things in the past. Now we cannot help redoing, refeeling them here and now, as if it were all actually happening to us.

Nevertheless, something has changed. In the furnace of theatrical involvement we are re-forged, reformed. Our own guilt, anger, resentment, jealousy and pride, as well as our pity and fear, are exorcised by the willingness to internalise the image of such things on behalf of others, who confront us in the play. The unique contribution of theatre to the exploration of human experience consists in the way in which it presents its images of truth. It may well be that some of the images that make up the true content of the drama do not depend entirely upon theatrical distance for their transforming power, as they implement in themselves a deeper kind of sharing than that represented within the conscious awareness of audience and actor – one that is mediated by the archetypes of the collective unconscious, the primary forms that govern the psyche, the 'most fundamental patterns of human existence', which manifest themselves in physical, social, linguistic, aesthetic and spiritual modes (1983b, 3). Even so, whatever may be communicated at conscious or unconscious level by the intrinsic imagery of action, character and setting, it is the presented play's fundamental identity as the place of cathartic identification that makes it an unforgettable experience of human relationship, a *locus classicus* of disclosed meaning, requiring and permitting a gift of self to other that is painful and renewing. Theatre is the archetypal expression of relationship-in-separation, the point at which souls touch each other and in doing so rediscover *themselves*.

And so we return to the question proposed in the last chapter. Should theatre be a way of teaching or of preaching? Or should it be the means whereby all preachers and teachers are gloriously murdered? Brecht aims at clarity or instruction; striving to avoid 'that literal and prosaic imitation which reaches perfection in a juggling of the sense by which the copy is mistaken for the original' (1965, note to *Die Mutter*). In this he is reacting directly against Aristotle's claim that theatre lives by emotional symbiosis, the power of feeling to arouse feeling. As one who preached a non-poetic, or even anti-poetic gospel, Brecht wished his sermons to be delivered in as prosaic a way as possible, his aim being education rather than any kind of conversion: and he viewed the theatre of catharsis with the good Socialist's horror of commercial exploitation: 'Like a businessman / investing money in a concern you suppose the spectator invests / feeling in the hero – he wants to get it back / if possible doubled' (quoted in Willett, 1960, 119). Businessmen and preachers have the same intention as businessmen – to entrap people into what appears to be a transaction aimed a mutual advantage, a genuine sharing of benefits, but is in fact an imposition of power aimed at self aggrandisement of one kind or another – social, economic or spiritual.

According to Brecht, Aristotelian theatre plays into the hands of those who would impose their own selfish intentions on others because it necessarily involves *a surrender of selfishness* on the part of the spectators, a willingness to allow themselves to feel on behalf of the personages presented to them in the play. The audience's emotions 'are disengaged from the petty interests of self...' (Butcher, 1951, 261, 6). This is certainly an open invitation to exploitation and the abuse of personal freedom, taking the form expected from those whose intention it is to play systematically on the feelings of others, whether they are advertisers or evangelists.

In fact, the contrast between Brechtian and Aristotelian theatre is not as stark as this, in the sense that the former's intentions are not able to be carried out to the extent that he would have wished owing to the fundamental nature of dramatic presentation. Manipulative theatre is not simply the theatre of illusion, nor is a theatre which succeeds in promoting freedom of thought and feeling simply one which honestly proclaims its own theatricality. The human imagination tends to function in accordance with its own dialectic, perversely shunning the emotionally explicit and actually thriving on the difficulties placed upon it by the *verfremdungseffekte*, the systematic erection of barriers against identification. The fact is, if we are carefully and scrupulously protected from the suggestion that we ought, from reasons of common humanity or personal experience, to feel a particular emotion, we are considerably more likely to feel it than if we are either instructed to suspend our disbelief or skilfully manipulated into believing. We may put up with being told what to think, but we tend to react strongly against being told what we must not feel. Identification represents a psychological position which is eagerly defended. Having overcome the barriers which divide person from person, and which in the theatre do so quite literally, even geographically, we are unwilling to retreat into our former isolation. As Grossvogel says, 'Once (the spectator) is asked to put flesh on the bare bones of a debate, the flesh will usually be his own, seldom the author's' (1962, 18). The very nature of the dramatic process is hypnotic. If it were not, Brecht would not have had to devote a lifetime of writing and coaching to neutralize its effects (Grossvogel, 1962, 18). Even so, it is at least doubtful that he ever really managed it! In the theatrical setting, to remind us of acting is to remind us of ourselves.

This brings us to Artaud, whose 'Theatre of Cruelty' seems to run counter to much that we have been saying about theatre up to now. At least one dimension of the 'cruelty' imagined by Artaud concerns the relationship between author and audience – between those presenting the play and the message that they intend to transmit, and the audience who, it is traditionally assumed, will make themselves open to receive their communication, of which theatre is the medium. Artaud does not agree. Theatre is not any kind of intervening condition between different understandings of the world, nor is it a world of its own, designed specifically to provide a safe meeting place for strangers, whom it enables to communicate by using the shared language of human experience. Traditional explanations of theatre lay great stress on the idea of a medium for encounter, some thing or condition which is safely interposed between realities – the known and the unknown, the familiar and the frightening, the reassuring and the challenging, the 'here' and the 'there'. Theatre is only ever seen as a transitional object in which a construct achieves spiritual significance at the locus of authentic human feelings and relationships.

Artaud has no time for this at all. Theatre, he says, is not a medium, but a *double*: 'it must present everything in love, crime, war and madness' (trans. 1970, 65). In other words it must make itself the equal of life. For him, the characters in a play are its subjects, not its presenters or demonstrators. Acting is the expression of a life-force which is both 'irrational and gratuitous' (trans. 1970, 65). As such it defies or even abolishes mere imitation. Because the things that are done and said, asserted and endured in the play are inherently real, anything that attempts to protect us from their force by interposing itself between us and them, detracts from their power to recreate us in their image. This is true of all kinds of explanation or commentary, any meta-message which aims at providing distance between ourselves and the impact of what is happening to us. Where theatre allows itself to be a channel for something – anything – *apart from the event itself*, it betrays its true being and neglects its unique contribution to human existence. Theatre's purpose is to expand life, not simply mirroring our reality but extending and completing it by putting it in touch with the original from which it derives its authority and force: 'If in fact we raise the question of the origins of and *raison d'être* (or primordial necessity) of the theatre, we find, metaphysically, the materialization, or rather the exteriorization of a kind of essential drama' (Artaud, trans. 1958, 50–51, in Derrida, 1978, 248,9).

The aim of author, director and actor is to increase the impact of the life force by embodying it in actions and events, gestures and statements that express rather than imitate life. It provides arbitrary and decisive interventions into the material of living which allow its inherent expressiveness and power to exceed our expectations to leap forth and violently shatter our attempts to control it through assimilating it to what we already know and feel. Acting is 'real' because it clings to the nature of the act itself and does not become expended, lost, denied: 'the image of a crime presented in the right stage conditions is something infinitely more dangerous to the mind than if the same crime were committed in life', for 'far from imitating life, theatre communicates wherever it can with pure forces' (Artaud, trans. 1970, 65, 62). Derrida quotes lines from a poem dating from Artaud's last years: 'The theatre is a passionate overflowing / a frightful transfer of forces / from body / to body / This transfer cannot be reproduced twice' (1978, 240).

For Artaud, the most valuable thing about theatre is its urgency. Theatre possesses an implacable urge towards embodiment, striving to take on the flesh of all those it embraces, be they audience or performers. As Derrida puts it 'We can distinguish "cruelty" as "necessity and vigor"' (1978, 238). This is the violence of theatre's urge to be itself by obliterating all traces of the life from which it is derived; which is why Derrida talks of 'parricide'. To allow any one individual dominance over what will happen on stage is drastically to limit the possibility of theatre. Authors, directors, actors impose their presence not to empower the theatrical happening, but to drain it of immediacy and hence of life. Theatre must be allowed to free itself from this dominance. The act of parricide is undertaken to protect the source of life by removing any kind of rival authority able to extinguish its primitive and original force. It is a healing murder.

Cruel theatre will 'no longer re-present a present that exists elsewhere and prior to it, a present whose plenitude would be older than it, absent from it, and rightfully capable of doing without it' (Derrida, 1978, 237). This is an event to be experienced as itself, and not to be registered and compared, evaluated in the light of something else, however distinguished. Theatre's nature and function stands forth as that of freedom: we are liberated from the past, and established in the present. Space and time are recreated here, and instead of the symbolism of an absence we are confronted by the presence of a reality that is *ourself*, ourself as we really are, instead of being reminded of our life as we are used to identifying it, in the familiar forms that we have adopted from elsewhere, and which, in conscience, do not actually belong to us at all. We are reborn in the spontaneity of our natural, unmodified humanity.

In order to prevent the interposition of any intermediate mental processes designed to lessen the impact of what is happening, cruel theatre depends on the most immediate means of communication possible. It substitutes confrontation for suggestion, movement and gesture for words. It lives through its rhythms, patterns and contrasts; its metaphors and revelations, repulsions and inducements, all of which are living symbols of human experience not encased in words. Above all, these symbols must be clear and recognisable. Words, if they are used at all, should be employed *as gesture rather than argument.* 'Theatre can reinstruct those who have forgotten the communicative power of gesture, because a gesture contains its own energy, and there are still human beings in theatre to reveal the power of these gestures' (Artaud, 1970, 61).

Gesture is preferred to speech as a symbol of the soul because words used as signs of feelings or ideas are inextricably tied in with the ways we are accustomed to interpreting them so as to be resonant in the theatrical sense; an aesthetic mystical distance must be preserved between concrete form and spiritual reality. Thus, the symbols of cruel theatre should be somewhat grotesque or outlandish so that they cannot be confused with anything which would distract from the as yet unknown realities to which we are impelled, as to the source of our most profound psychological conflicts. The 'natural, occult equivalent of the dogma we no longer believe', this theatre 'reveals their dark powers and hidden strength to men, urging them to take a nobler more heroic stance in the face of destiny' (Artaud, 1970, 22).

How are we to take all this? The 'cruelty' Artaud demands does not completely obliterate the theatre we are used to. Indeed it lays bare aspects of theatre which we have sensed all along, and often conveniently forgotten about. We are driven to the conclusion that Artaud looked to the theatre for release from the schizoid awareness which seeks to systematize experience as a way of defending itself from contact with life. Theatre represents his vision of health and human completeness; not because it is real or final truth about life, but because it itself *is* life, human life, in its full potentiality. His rationale for this is unconventional. It is that, like art, life is really an imitation. Herein lies the authenticity of theatre as a genuine expression – of humanness. 'Art is not the imitation of life. Life is the imitation of a transcendent principle with which art restores communication' (1970, 4: 310). Because it brings us back into contact with an otherness in relationship with which we may discover our true identity, theatre is inalienably and fundamentally therapeutic. Artaud's approach bears witness to an existential transformation which, like Aristotle's, proceeds from a redemption experience undergone in the theatre.

The 'symptoms' of this resemble those of any other peak experience (to use Maslow's expression (1962)) of a mystical, or transcendent kind, involving the resolution of painful psychological discords, the submergence of negative feeling beneath a tide of positive emotion which carries everything before it. The self no longer feels cut off, lost, resentful, an outsider, a mistake; and a single note now emerges from a discord of thundering counterpoints. In this way, by bringing about a kind of Hegelian synthesis of conflicting forces, theatre puts us in touch with the infinite, which is not a force but a unifying presence. Of all modern writers about theatre, Artaud is the most aware of the paradoxical 'truth through illusion' of the dramatic event and the essential obliqueness of theatrical mechanisms. Just as it is impossible to create genuine theatre by the direct imitation of reality, it is pointless to try to capture its spirit in the language of straightforward description. Both theatre and life are fabrications put together in the attempt to achieve the kind of wholeness and authenticity which will always elude us as long as we pretend we are not pretending. (Artaud and Goffman would have found much to agree about!)

As the testimony of one who looked for an answer to his own alienation and that of all creation in theatre, *The Theatre and its Double* (Artaud, trans. 1970) is a very revealing text. It is a characteristic of the schizoid awareness that the meaning which sustains people and things in relationship – what William James refers to as the 'noetic' element in our experience – seems to have been drained away, leaving everything and everyone stranded in a condition of isolated incompleteness in which the world appears a grotesque collection of random and irrelevant objects, a kind of lumber room of the spirit. The passion and conviction of Artaud's vision of the theatre; his certainty that here, in the 'communicative delirium' of an intense theatrical event, is the remedy for the sickness which divides us and shuts reality up behind a wall of thoughts that thought cannot penetrate, constitute the most impressive evidence of the healing force of drama. Artaud's letters provide evidence that *The Theatre and Its Double* is not merely a collection of writings about theatre, or even the record of successive attempts at the analysis of theatrical experience; it is an intensely personal document in which a threatened and oppressed sensibility describes the terms and circumstances of its rehabilitation.

Like Nietzsche, Artaud sees the stage as a place of violent and primitive Dionysiac forces. However, what the former perceives as a process of taming and controlling, the latter experiences as a means of liberation. The theatrical encounter gives life because it involves participation in the pre-categorical event which generates life itself. It possesses a particular function of exorcism, breaking up established patterns of life, which it reveals as destructive of our potential for genuine human growth. Theatre releases conflicts, disengages powers, liberates possibilities: 'if these possibilities and these powers are dark, it is not the fault of theatre, but of life' (Artaud, 1970, 21).

The symbolism of cruel theatre, then, is powerful but obscure. Its meaning is lived rather than interpreted. The feeling of involvement in the reality of human life is Artaud's principal objective and dominating symbol. In *The Theatre and Its Double* we have powerful evidence of Artaud's longing for delivery from his own alienation. In his search for a theatre 'which events will not exceed', he expresses the longing for human contact characterising an awareness that is agonizingly sensitive to its own isolation. Contact must be immediate, unmediated by any kind of commentary, any standing back from itself and the event in which it finds completion.

On the other hand, the mediation which Artaud violently resists is that of the explanatory, the commentary that modifies statements, 'putting them in context'; it is not to be confused with the underlying circumstances in which the theatrical meeting takes place, in which the medium is not an intrusive presence but an enabling and welcoming absence. The creation of aesthetic distance in the play's presentation is the means whereby freedom and possibility are asserted; it goes out of its way to make no comment, draw no conclusion. You are safe here, it says; where you stand there is nothing to fear. You can afford to open yourself to anything that may happen to you in these circumstances. Demands, threats, restrictions; censure, accusation, self-blame; futility, impotence, despair; anger, ruthlessness, destruction, even chaos itself (particularly chaos!), everything negative and self-defeating, impersonal or anti-human, is kept at a distance; not by argument, which invariably bears witness to what it seeks to deny by the action of denying it, but by the symbolism of encounter and mutuality. Somehow the theatrical symbol clears a space for people and things *as they are* – free from the rationalisations that tend to confuse linguistic *signs* (spoken descriptions or metaphors) with their *reference*, thus destroying the otherness of the other by including it within the known and understood. The symbol produces emptiness, not information; but this emptiness exerts its own force on us, and we are drawn towards a reality without words or thoughts to protect ourselves. Artaud speaks of 'a vacuum in thought...lucid language which prevents this emptiness also prevents poetry appearing in thought' (1970, 53). For him, distance occurs within the symbol: what is interposed between person and person, actor and spectator, actor and author, author and spectator – is a gap designed to be filled, a separation moving towards its own resolution. It is this freedom which beckons and encourages us.

Artaud and Brecht agree that theatre begins with an empty space and proceeds to fill it with new life. The purpose of the free-standing theatrical symbol, the sign that cannot ever be confused with its reference within the world of ideas and reasons, is to assert and establish an unexplained, unassimilated space in our awareness: to help us temporarily *not* to know. Theatrical symbols do not permit us to *understand*, in the sense of including things within our personal way of construing the world, but to experience the unknown without defensiveness so that we can move forward to the encounter without fear. Theatre distracts us from our well-thought-out positions, even those that are taken up by the people most intimately involved, be they actors, director or author. By involving us in its own world through the psychological force of its images and the special circumstances governing their *presentation outside argument*, in a universe structured to disarm us, cruel theatre 'releases conflicts, disengages powers, liberates possibilities'. This kind of theatre can be a draught from the well-spring of life. Our parched awareness is refreshed by life at its source – we are united and renewed. Our defences against one another are broken down and we are restored to the relationship with being which our intellect resists.

This, then, is Artaud's 'Theatre of Cruelty'. As an event it is philosophically unanalysable, and our attempt to look at it intellectually reduces it to useless schemata. Artaud himself finds it impossible to describe without resorting to poetry; and indeed, in its violence it is precisely that. Its poetic symbolism sets out to destroy the power exerted by a prose which can only describe its subject rather than embody it, and in so doing, reduces what it describes to another version of itself. According to Artaud, theatre is essentially an open-ended symbol, leading not following; consequently it must be violent. It must be 'a theatre which is not overshadowed by events, but arouses deep echoes within us' (1970, 64).

It has turned out to be something of a vain hope. Theatre requires some kind of plot, and plots are open to interpretation and re-interpretation. The violent happenings and assaults on the audience's feelings which characterise our naive attempts at producing 'cruel' theatre tend too often to send us in pursuit of an explanation as to why these things are going on, and we look in vain to Artaud himself for any kind of dramatic text which we could copy and so arrive at the passion of an unmediated meeting with others, and, consequently, ourselves. Fortunately, the simplest and quietest play, if it manages to speak as itself, may involve us in the kind of salutary and shocking re-discovery of life that Artaud means when he talks of cruelty. It is also true that writing does not have to be practical in order to be a source of inspiration.

In *The Theatre and Its Double*, Artaud drew attention to the healing power exerted by what might be called the core dramatic event upon his divided sensibility, his shattered perception of the world and himself in it. We should not be surprised if his experience of renewal sounds more dramatic than the emotional purging proposed by Aristotle. However, when it comes down to it, both are speaking about the same thing, achieved in the same way. The notion of contact and detachment, danger and safety, on which catharsis depends is present in a doctrine of theatre which lays the greatest stress on an experience of direct, unmediated encounter, just as it is in a view which locates aesthetic distance in the actual physical separation of actor and spectator. Artaud locates the place and time of encounter *within the theatrical symbol itself*. Here, in the play's 'cruel' heart, we are presented with the ruthless truthfulness which alone can draw us together and heal our alienation. If what Artaud says is true, the bolder our symbolism, the more healing it will be for those who have been damaged by environments that are emotionally isolating or cognitively confusing. What is certain, however, is that the principal bearer of this symbolism, the target on which it is focused and the sharp, cutting edge of its impact, remains the living person of the actor.

CHAPTER 7

As If and Healing

The notion of the healing effect of the dramatic 'as if' whereby we put ourselves in someone else's place, thinking and feeling as if we actually were that person has been explored by psychologists and psychotherapists. From a psychoanalytic point of view it is connected with the fundamental experience of transfer of personality whereby memories are awakened at an unconscious level by someone who takes on the role of the person whom the memories really concern. The analyst becomes, not me myself, certainly, but someone who played, and plays a key role in my personal history: someone who, because they are so integral to my psychological life, is crucial to my sense of personhood... As I relive my story, the analyst 'becomes' the father with whom I came to identify. I rediscover him within the present relationship with a vivid conscious awareness which draws its force from feelings that have long been disowned and consigned to unconsciousness. The scenario of analysis is familiar because its central character, the analyst, has become through a long and difficult process of identification, an aspect of myself. The paternalism implied in the traditional psychotherapeutic settings strikes a powerful chord in our 'emotional memory' and we find ourselves ready to collude in a carefully constructed revival of an ancient, painstakingly forgotten drama.

Freud himself describes the process whereby the patient comes to regard the doctor 'as if' he (the doctor) were actually his (the patient's) own father as 'A transference of feeling upon the personality of the physician'. [This] 'was ready and prepared in the patient and was transferred upon the physician at the occasion of the analytical treatment.' He goes on to explain that 'His feelings do not originate in the present situation and they are not really deserved by the personality of the physician, but they repeat what has happened to him once before in his life' (1925, 475, 7). The patient is enabled by the similarity in role relationship between the one he had as a child with his father, and the present circumstances which require an identical submissiveness to authority experienced as total, to recapture and relive the feelings he had then: not only love, but anger, frustration and resentment, the envy and guilt associated with Oedipal conflict. This is not an exclusively male reaction; we are using the masculine pronoun here because it is Freud's usage. Nor is it exclusively a hostile one; 'positive transference' results in "feelings of liking, solicitude and loving towards the helper" (Watkins, 1983, 206). The point to be registered is that the therapist–client relationship, being one of dominance–submission, re-activates the negative feelings about such relationships that we carry with us for most of our lives and first experience in childhood.

Equally significant, however, is the reason why such feelings erupt at this particular point and in these circumstances. It is because in the therapeutic relationship we are encouraged to reveal things about ourselves which we have trained ourselves not to recognise. The client–analyst relationship is a special kind of social setting, very safe because it is completely accepting. Reassured by our sense of security, the security we longed for as children and did not always experience, we indulge our long-postponed rage. Thus we are defensive and aggressive, dominant and submissive, safe and exposed at the same time, and achieve the emotional balance that Scheff associates with catharsis, by which we are set free from ungoverned psychological pressure exerted from one direction only.

Later in his career, Freud completed the picture of an interchange of repressed feelings between the two 'actors in the transferential drama' by isolating a reaction on the therapist's part which he described as 'counter-transference', and which was motivated by the patient's ability, within the special therapeutic setting, to re-activate negative feelings which the therapist had repressed. Freud does not elaborate on the reasons for this reversal; the logical explanation appears to be that the situation in itself is enough to re-activate hidden or repressed feelings on the part of everyone involved. Certainly C.G. Jung regarded the therapeutic relationship as a setting for unconscious experiences with a wider symbolic reference than Freud was able to accept. For Jung the images that surfaced in therapy concerned much more than the private memories of either client or therapist. In therapy, the client came into contact with profound truth about life itself; the healing identification is with a less tangible presence than a medical/paternal one – less tangible, but more powerful. Rather than deriving the unconscious from the conscious via the action of repression as Freud does, Jung regards the unconscious as primary, the origin of all our understanding about reality, the 'whole way in which we organize the world we live in'. ('I was on excellent terms with him [Freud] until I had the idea that certain things were symbolical – symbolical, that is, of a metaphysical truth undreamt of in psychoanalytical theory' (1968, 140).) For Jung 'as if' signifies identifying unconscious truth and consciously allying with it in our conscious lives. Actual identification with the therapist was valuable only as a way of helping this to happen.

All the same, Freud laid great stress on the importance of client–therapist transference, regarding it as potentially the most powerful process in psychoanalysis. His followers have usually supported him in this, finding in the re-activation of emotions concerning 'important figures' in the client's personal history the most effective way of achieving the relationship of genuine mutuality which alone brings psychological healing. Writing in 1958, W.R.D. Fairbairn says: 'What I understand by "the relationship between the analyst and the patient" is not just the relationship involved in the transference, but the total relationship existing between the patient and analyst as persons' (1958, 374–385). During the last twenty years, a good deal of attention has been paid to this 'therapeutic alliance' of analyst and patient. Moras and Strupp, for example, writing in 1982, found that mutuality, relatedness and trust were of crucial importance in establishing a therapeutic alliance of patient and analyst which would permit short-term therapy to succeed (1982, 405–9). Others have stressed the need for conscious psychological identification apart from unconscious transference. Somehow the first must develop into the second. Clients need to be able consciously to re-identify with an alternative parental figure who can 'provide the matrix (sic) for a corrective emotional experience by being…different from the parent, by being committed to the patient and by trying to understand' (Shapiro, 1983, 50–60; Holmes, 1965).

Psychotherapies derived from psychoanalysis and from Jungian analytical psychology tend towards the idea of meeting the patient or client on his or her own terms, using symbolism that she or he finds personally reassuring and liberating. This means working hard to create an atmosphere specifically designed for the natural expression of spontaneous impulses. Outstanding in this direction is the client-centred therapy of Carl Rogers:

> 'The therapist perceives the client's self as the client has known it, and accepts it. He perceives the contradictory aspects which have been denied to awareness, and accepts these too as part of the client… Thus it is that the client, experiencing in another an acceptance of both these aspects of himself can take towards himself the same attitude' (1976, 41)

For client-centred therapy, healing consists 'in experiencing the self in a wide range of ways in an emotionally meaningful relationship with the therapist' (1976, 172). Rogers stresses the need for clients to receive permission from the therapist to play a succession of different roles. The emotional security of his or her regard and concern will give them the necessary confidence to 'be' a range of other selves, leaving the known and familiar for what has often been thought about but never actually lived. Experiment with self-hood takes place in the secure framework of a secure relationship with an acceptable, and accepting, authority. 'Every aspect of himself which he (the client) exposes is equally accepted.' This is necessary, because if the client is threatened he or she 'may further distance the symbolization of experience' – that is, withdraw into their old, familiar 'shell' and refuse to continue the experiment (1976, 194).

The setting in which therapist–client encounter will take place is widely held to be of the very greatest significance both for reviving childhood reality and for reflecting someone's view of themselves with regard to other people with whom they are in contact in their daily lives within the present. Because of its nature, the psychotherapeutic relationship requires a high degree of self-consciousness, both from the therapist and the client. In order for it to work properly, the healing role must be clearly defined. It must be convincing enough to resonate with the client's expectations, which, unrealistic though they may sometimes be, have brought him or her along in the first place. Similarly, there must be an answering role in the drama for the client. He or she must be 'the person who is going to be helped and healed'. This role involves some things that she or he finds aversive: the need to admit inability to heal oneself, for example, plus the obligation to confront aspects of life, and of the self, that are painful and frightening, and to permit the discovery of things up to now kept hidden even from one's own private view (McDougall, 1986). Worst of all, the patient or client's role means adopting a passive and dependent position as the sick person in the plot. Nevertheless, if it is to be convincing both to healer and healed, the action of the drama must be recognisable. It must have roles that, however much they are modified in the course of therapy, transmit the inalienable meaning within a drama about a healing encounter. This is a real event, not merely a theory. For 'as if' to become operational at a personal level involves a particular kind of awareness, one which is self-conscious and reflexive in the presence of the other. Put this into the language of real events, and we have drama – maybe not officially, but always by implication. To create any kind of shared imaginative world requires a place to meet, a structure for encounter, a set of literal conditions that is transformed by drama into a figurative meaning.

Dramatic approaches to psychotherapy are effective because they refer to a model of human experience which is fundamentally truthful. Drama presents life experience as relation-in-separation, where the separatedness permits and constitutes the relatedness. The specific model of human understanding is one described by Stephen Pepper as *contextual*, the notion of the 'act in context'. The contextual approach is concerned with solving problems experientially rather than theoretically. It has more to do with phenomenology than science. According to Pepper, life can only really be understood in a way that safeguards its personal character by paying attention, not to things or people themselves, or even to processes of interaction involving people or things (or people and things), but to what he calls 'the historical moment'. This does not mean a past event, 'one that is dead and has to be exhumed'; such an approach has more to do with the objectivity of science than the inter-subjectivity of personal experience. On the contrary, the history referred to here is our awareness of the present moment: 'The event alive in the present…when it is going on *now*, the dynamic, dramatic, active event' (1942, 232). It is the living quality of events as they take place among people that makes time real to us. Drama represents. Even when it refers to the past it does so in the language of our involvement in all that is taking place in the here and now. It is the past – or the present or future – as we are living it now, as if it were happening at this particular moment. We do not stand outside the flux of time and our own involvement in it in order to make our judgements of the event as impersonal as possible. Indeed, the more impersonal we are, the more we absent ourselves from the reality of what is going on. Even if we bring our reasoning intellect with us, it is certainly not all that we bring.

The contextual hypothesis takes account of the pattern of relationships embodied in each moment of reflexive interpersonal experience. Life is understood by means of dramatic involvement, not rational analysis. In *The Leaves of Spring* (1972), Aaron Esterson draws attention to the difference between the kind of human knowing which refers to the interplay of actual behaviours, and the kind that 'explains' people in terms of psychological processes that condition their behaviour on an impersonal, mechanistic level; the kind of knowing that characteristically finds solutions to intractable interpersonal problems in the diagnosis of mental illness.

> 'An observer of others may adopt either of these two stances. He may see the pattern of events to be due primarily to a mechanically determined sequence, or he may see it as primarily the expression of *the intentions of the persons comprising the system*. The movement of an arm may be seen primarily as a pattern of flexion and extension of

muscles and joints, or it may be seen primarily as striking a blow.'
(Esterson, 1972, 212. Our emphasis)

These two ways of interpreting the same human action, either impersonally, as the result of the working of a physiological machine, or personally, expressing a human intention concerning a social relationship, are described by Esterson and Laing as 'process' and 'praxis'. Human beings can never really be understood by and as themselves if our concerns with the former distort our appreciation of the latter.

As the sphere within which human intentions are symbolised, praxis involves much more than simple interactive behaviour. Human intentionality refers to a global, contextual realm of experience, as we use our bodies and the products of our minds in symbolic ways as well as directly instrumental ones. For us, the movement of the arm which does not make actual physical contact with someone else's chin may create a more permanent and far-reaching impression because of its expressiveness as a human gesture than it would have done if it had 'connected'. As a symbolic gesture its connections may be infinitely wider and more important. It is as the realm in which human meaning is transmitted through various kinds of codified extensions of the human gesture that praxis comes into its own. This in turn depends on our ability to stand, as it were, apart from ourselves and look at ourselves 'as if' we were somebody else who is receiving the symbols we are transmitting. Relationship and the communication of meaning are synonymous, and the precondition of both is reflexive self-awareness. The study of oneself and other people requires us to include ourselves as part of the situation we are studying. As Esterson says:

> 'An interpersonal relationship is one in which each, while relating to each, implicitly experiences each as experiencing himself relating to the other, and as experiencing the possibility of so relating, and as experiencing the possibility of knowing the form and style of the relation they are each making with each other' (that is, the degree of intimacy and its social significance). (1972, 213, 214)

If such a complicated form of awareness can be represented effectively with reference to a recognisable social network, rather than simply the *idea* of such a network, the result is bound to be a form of drama. Therapy will take place dialectically and involve a cast of people, of whom the therapist is one (1972, 221–230). Its logic will be that of social truth in action, in the experience of the interplay of persons in relationship, rather than the observation of individuals in an isolation which, in aiming at objectivity, deprives them of the humanity it sets out to understand.

The idea of a 'theatre of the self and others' has assumed an important place in psychotherapy. It finds its clearest expression in the work of Jacob Moreno, the inventor of sociodrama and psychodrama. Moreno moved away from the psychoanalytic preoccupation with the first years of a client's life and concentrated on the network of immediate relationships in which he or she is involved within the present situation. For Moreno, the 'presenting problem' is the actual locus of concern. He arrived at this somewhat radical conclusion through the discovery that essential information about an individual's emotional life is revealed by concentrating on the social interaction among a group of clients of which he or she is a member. Instead of attempting to discover unconscious motivation for present behaviour, Moreno turned his attention to the knots tied in the conscious ego by our efforts to keep our balance among the conflicting demands and pressures of the social networks that sustain us but also distort our judgement, circumscribe our awareness and – most important of all – restrict our freedom to be ourselves. We are pulled this way and that in the present by other people. The picture is too complex, we are too vulnerable to changes not of our own making, for us to look clearly at what is happening to us.

Moreno used sociodramatic techniques to demonstrate and clarify his clients' awareness of their interpersonal relationships. A space was specially set aside in order for individual clients to position themselves in ways that demonstrated the 'closeness' or 'distance' that they felt towards one another. The arrangement of physical bodies in space acted as a dramatic indicator of social meanings, and consequently of individual interpretations of personal experience. Individual clients 'cast' one another in roles representing classes and groups within society, so that the finished sociogram would bring home their personal view of wider issues affecting themselves or their group.

These actual pictures possessed an unexpected logic. Moreno noticed that groups arranged themselves as if they already possessed the information necessary for an accurate representation of one another's ideas, attitudes and feelings. He came to the conclusion that the members of a group communicate with one another in unspoken ways. How otherwise was it possible to account for the fact that 'real sociograms differ significantly from chance sociograms' (Moreno, 1959, 10)? In other words, the tableaux and the diagrams reproduced from them, revealed the existence of a channel of communication which was invisible and inaudible but somehow managed to draw like-minded people together so that they assumed a kind of group personality. Moreno identified this with what he called *tele*. Tele differs from the unconscious transference of affect, being more like shared empathy: 'We must assume that some real process in one person's life situation is sensitive and corresponds to some real process in another person's life situation' (Moreno 1937).

With the development of psychodrama itself, tele became the principle theatrical underpinning of an approach to individual psychotherapy, involving the systematic use of role-reversal to exploit the possibilities for greater inter-personal insight and acceptance of oneself and other people. Psychodrama involves the interchange of roles among members of a group who represent the social network of a particular person who is present. This person then becomes the central character, or 'protagonist', of the presentation of his or her own life-drama, which undergoes successive modification as those involved exchange roles so that they can act out their own interpretation of the situation. In this way, everybody present has the opportunity to present the drama in the way that they themselves see it, in the light of their imaginative insight into 'what it must be like to be so and so, in such a situation'. The presence of shared understanding and acceptance within the group gives an amazing intensity to the drama, which becomes a melting pot for individual experiences of the most personal kind. We are set free from considerations of personal defensiveness by being directed towards someone else's situation. We are personally involved in someone else's drama.

This is the cathartic event of theatre reduced to its simplest and most basic form, in which a group recreates its own personal experiences by taking on the courage and strength of others, a courage and strength set free by sharing. The courage to become involved, to associate one's own struggle with someone else's and draw strength from the release of pent-up emotion and the surrender of defensiveness does not depend here on the kind of distancing provided by the division of audience from actors. The vital sense of security which it seems we must have before we can find the courage to allow others' pain to encounter, and so modify our own, is discovered in the action of the tele which flows 'within' the group and gives it a sense of unity, mutual acceptance and intuited courage.

The way that tele operates, however, is by means of role-reversal. This is crucial to Moreno's theory. The love that heals in psychodrama is

> 'A meeting of lives; eye to eye, face to face. And when you are near I will tear your eyes out and place them instead of mine, and you will tear my eyes out and place them instead of yours, then I will look at you with your eyes and you will look at me with mine.' (1959, 11)

Thus, tele provides a medium for 'as if'. In this, it corresponds to artistic experience. While appearing to be the opposite of distance it is a mediating dimension that separates and unites. At the same time, the adoption of a dramatic 'frame' expressed in a defined acting space underlines Moreno's belief in the necessity for structures which are able to contain and channel the spontaneity produced by tele.[1] Distance, then, is the presence of tele in its contained and focused form.

The action of reversing roles is personally validating in that by attempting to perceive as if I were you, not only do I distance myself from my own private pre-occupations, breaking the chain with which I habitually tie myself to myself, but I rediscover my own sense of self as I perceive myself to be the object of your awareness. To this extent I quit myself in order to look back at myself. Where we both do this we reinforce each other's sense of existing as persons. By the same token, the imaginative switch dislodges the current rules about role relationships within a hierarchy of social positions. In psychodrama, considerations of superiority and inferiority, dominance and submission are continually being reversed: 'The psychoanalytic rule that the situation of analysis "involves a superior and a subordinate" is replaced by the psychodramatic rule that every participant is superior or subordinate according to the role which he plays in the psychodramatic production' (1959, 96).

In fact the technique of role reversal refers directly back to the striking improvement that Moreno himself noticed in his relationship with his own small son as a result of playing 'I'll be you and you be me' games. The quality of the insight into the relationship of self and other provided by this simple formula came as something of a revelation, transforming his ideas about what psychotherapy was and how it should be practiced. The dramatic format of psychodrama, being a specialised form of play, provides the necessary security for the imaginative appropriation of one another's experience. It makes contact with a desire to explore the imaginative experience of 'being someone else' which can be seen to characterise childhood and to form one of the main, if not the main ways in which human beings adapt to changes in the environment and store up insights which will guide their future behaviour. The need to participate in other people's *relationships with other people* is a potent force in the resolution of Oedipal conflict, as the developing

---

1   Moreno, J. L., 1959, 103: 'The greater mobility and flexibility of the format-free therapies has some disadvantages...the tendency to be intuitive and interpretative makes it difficult to communicate with other therapists and to compare with them what happens in a session.'

child learns ways of practising how to appreciate and then share points of view previously experienced as conflicting with its own.

This ability to mirror other people's experience, learned when we first became aware of our own separate selfhood, characterises every succeeding period of life. It is not something we ever grow out of, but is a 'light to our path' to the end of our lives. As Moreno says, 'Man's imagination will not quit the eternal child in him' (1959, 154).[2] Thus psychodrama depends entirely on the artistic discretion of the willed human imagination. It requires 'the full involvement of the actor in the act.' (1959, 215) As with all drama, its ability to heal depends on its emotional authenticity. Those who take part in it on its own terms are 'existentially validated' (to use Moreno's phrase) by an emotionally truthful experience which accepts their testimony as valuable and legitimate. Psychodrama's terms include the acceptance of individual people as they are, on their own terms, as 'the patient becomes the chief guide in the research about him as well as in his cure' (1959, 216). Other psychotherapeutic approaches, notably gestalt therapy, structure the healing relationship in a dramatic way in order to re-connect clients in a non-linguistic way with parts of the self that they have denied (Perls, 1973).

Dramatherapy as such depends very much on role-distance – that is, on our freedom to exchange current roles and invent and adopt new ones. Although the protagonists of a psychodrama start off by presenting them-selves as themselves, during the course of the session they play a range of other people in order to achieve the distance from their customary role which they must have in order to identify ways of changing it or modifying it. Other members of the group, meanwhile, are engaged in taking on the role of others in the cast during the entire psychodrama. In *dramatherapy* as distinct from *psychodrama* the main approach tends to be in the invention of roles rather than their adoption from a ready made scenario such as the one represented by the actual life-circumstances of a member of the group. This involves a change in the way we think about roles, according to which we pay attention to their nature as constructs rather than as fixed elements within specific social situations. Instead of thinking in terms of changing a current role in order to have an effect on the social circumstances involved, we have to consider the notion of substituting an entirely new one, and so completely changing the circumstances. We must begin to think of our social role as something that we ourselves have invented, and can consequently re-invent.

---

2   cf J. Lacan, *Écrits: A Selection*, (trans. A. Sheridan, New York, Norton, 1977) and p.11, n2 of this book.

Here, personal construct psychology can help us by arguing convincingly that the way we behave in the world has a dramatic effect on the world as we perceive it; and the way we behave is a function, not of external facts, but of our own internal system of making personal sense of those facts. If we change the way we construe the world, we change the ways that we behave in it, and consequently the way others behave towards us. Subjectivity has a powerful effect on the 'objective facts'. They only assume this status when we allow them to do so, and we are at liberty to modify their factual nature, or even to remove it altogether, by bestowing the 'fact' of objectivity on an entirely different organisation of the perceptual evidence. Facts that have been argued – or even intuited – out of existence are no longer facts *for us*. George Kelly, who invented personal construct psychology called its underlying theory 'constructive alternativism'.

> 'Man looks at his world through transparent patterns or templates which he creates and then attempts to fit over the realities of which the world is composed... Let us give them the name of *constructs* that are tentatively tried on for size. They are ways of construing the world... We take the stand that there are always some *alternative constructions* available to choose among in dealing with the world.' (Kelly, 1955, 8, 15)

These 'personal constructs' are not simply ideas about ourselves thought up to suit our own inclinations. On the contrary, they are the way in which we take account of the subjectivity of other people in order to interact with them in ways that will be mutually satisfactory, mutually supportive. They are the building blocks of society, which can only exist if its members are able to make the imaginative leap of including constructs of other people's experi-ence – their pre-suppositions and expectations, attitudes and intentions, likes and dislikes, *ways of construing* – within their own personal construct systems. (Or, as Kelly expresses it: 'To the extent that one person construes the construction processes of another, he may play a role in a social process involving the other person' (1955, 95).)

Kelly himself made use of the paradigm of drama in what he called fixed role therapy. This was a practical adaptation of constructive alternativism for specifically therapeutic purposes, a way of embodying the freedom to invent oneself that he described. Fixed role therapy is genuinely theatrical in its conception in that it involves the systematic rehearsal of ways of behaving as if one had actually revised one's way of construing reality, so as to be able to make a real break with the past and see oneself – and be seen by others – as a different kind of person. The transformation in being was to be brought about by doing. According to constructive alternativism, it is we who make our present selves by deciding who we want to be. Roles can be made genuinely and authentically personal by getting used to them and 'making them our own': 'What would happen,' Kelly asked 'if we took the general view that what people do is a feature of what they *are*, that the extent to which a person *behaves* in a certain way is a measure of the extent to which he *is* that kind of person?' (1955, 363). The object of fixed role therapy was to provide people with the opportunity to practice behaving 'as if' their personal construct system were organised differently, and they had started to see the world in a way that was slightly different; different enough, that is, to affect their actual behaviour. In other words, attitudinal change was to be induced by overt behavioural change. It was anticipated that, because of the systematic nature of the way we construe whatever it is that happens to us, even a slight alteration of the criteria we use in order to make sense of things might have a noticeable effect on our outward lives. Now that we saw things in a new light, we would adjust our behavioural priorities, giving more importance to some courses of action and ways of reacting than we had done previously. In this way we would actually take on a new role, one specifically designed to function according to our modified construction system and to avoid the way of thinking that previously caused us, and others, trouble.

Both the rehearsal and performance of the new dramatic creation are more private than psychodrama. The transfer of personal role identity is a process carried out in order to convince an audience which to the end remains unconscious of being present at a performance. The script (that is, the new method of self-presentation) is prepared by therapist and client on the foundation of a self-characterisation written by the latter and rehearsed in the former's presence before being tried out in public. At first the new role is presented only in the most favourable circumstances; as time goes on and it grows more familiar to the client, it may be used more and more frequently, until at length it has become second nature:

> 'When the client shows signs, either in rehearsal or outside that he was just acting, the therapist may assume that…a process is in motion which tends to interweave the client's new role constructs with the fabric of his main construction system.' (Kelly, 1955, 410)

The idea that personal integrity requires the ability to choose one's own roles and the willingness to play them with complete conviction is central to personal construct psychology. In fixed role therapy, individual clients choose the direction in which they want to change and create a social role that will establish the changed behaviour that they envisage. The process of actual self-discovery is not so far reaching as it in psychodrama and there is no built in mechanism for producing catharsis. We are still in the realm of role-play rather than genuine theatre, although the experience of becoming involved in psychologically threatening social situations while sustaining an unfamiliar role increases the sense of personal distance and has been known to have had a decidedly cathartic effect. The really outstanding contribution made to drama based therapy by the fixed role approach lies in the opportunity it affords for existential encouragement and the rehearsal of personal possibilities.

> 'The [therapist's] job is to help people to create new hypotheses and to experiment with them as a means of growing. He does not tell people what they should eventually *be*, he only suggests what they may now *try out.*' (Kelly, 1955, 387)

Dramatherapy allies with the structural emphasis of theatre as this is reproduced in the client–therapist relationship. Role reversal and role invention both depend upon the strict definition of roles: Moreno clearly states that 'Spontaneity is a readiness of the subject to respond as required' (1959 in Fox 1987); in other words, to react creatively to structures. At another level, the processes of transference involved in our identification with people in plays require the presentation of well-defined, easily recognisable personages who have played significant roles in our lives. This is the clarity, flexibility and force that characterise 'as if' when it assumes the form of drama. In dramatherapy, structure promotes freedom and security gives rise to courage. The secure base for healing is a matter of territoriality as much as transferred feelings about the safety of personal relationships. At least, negative reactions to dependency upon the therapist/parent are taken up within the dramatic scenario to become a 'constructive alternative' to any kind of static and unproductive resentment and rivalry. The recognition of a space clearly marked out as one's own, in which one can live and grow, from which one can reach out and expand is drama's most obvious gift to therapy. An unconscious longing for childhood security may contribute to the force of a lesson consciously learned throughout life about the need to mark out one's own space to discover one's own outline, in order to be able to share selfhood with others. As a place to move out from, dramatherapy participates in the essence of drama.

Psychotherapeutic enactment is of two principal kinds; exposition and exploration. Expository enactment is concerned principally with enacting oneself, by which is meant the conscious demonstration of a person's own selfhood; how one experiences both oneself and others' experience of oneself. In other words, it reveals the 'I' and the 'me' in dramatic or theatrical form. Psychodrama belongs in this category, at least in its original or classical configuration. The explicitly contextual approach of psychodrama is developed in gestalt psychotherapy, which first emerged as a distinctive approach to psychotherapy in the 1950s in the work of Fritz Perls, whose theory of the nature of human functioning centred upon the process of interaction between the individual and his or her environment. The relationship between foreground and background in our way of picturing reality governs the kind of sense we make of ourselves and our world (Perls, Hefferstone, and Goodman 1973). The juxtaposition of people, things and ideas reflects their relative salience in our meaning-plan just as, in a dramatic presentation, certain people are made more or less important to the action of the play by the actual positions they occupy within the acting area. Acting things out has a dramatic effect on the way we see them, giving them a potentiality for movement that they never possessed in *verbal* descriptions of a particular state of affairs. The possibility of foreground and background changing places appears to be more realistic within an actual drama than in the two dimensional world of language. Enactment transforms linguistic events into processes, and in doing so presents us with a fuller and more complete version of the original reality than a client's description could do. According to I. and M. Polster, 'It is one way of keeping alive the words a person uses to characterize himself or someone else. Keeping his language connected to action permits feelings of change and growth' (Polster and Polster, 1975, 164).

Expository enactment of this kind brings clarity and flexibility to the therapeutic encounter: 'Through enactment the therapist has available an approximate reference structure. By comparing it with the client's verbal descriptions, the therapist has an example of the generalizations, deletions and distortions typical of the client,' who, through the drama, 'expresses possibilities which had been previously deleted'. At the same time, enactment presents the client's model of the world as an experience that is still alive and kicking rather than one that has been verbally defused for easy handling. There is less chance of leaving out things that still cause pain in the client, and which he or she would rather find ways of not mentioning – either to himself or anyone else: 'Portions of the client's model (of reality) which were vague and unfocused are clarified, as the enactment is a specific experience', and must somehow hang together as such (Bandler and Grinder, 1975, 164–5).

In what we have chosen to call exploratory enactment there is an equal clarity of focus, but it is directed elsewhere – not onto the client but onto someone else, not immediately presenting his experiential world, but drawing our attention towards a vivid fiction. Exploratory enactment involves taking a new role, modelled on another person. According to psychological principles which are to do with the way we form the personal alliances which structure our world-construction, this person is chosen to 'be' ourself during the course of the enactment, and to remain part of our experiential memory for some time afterwards, perhaps for the rest of our lives. Thus, dramatherapy is exploratory in a way that is literal and direct; we mentally explore someone else's experience. The psychological interaction which we have claimed to be characteristic of drama and theatre applies directly to mainstream dramatherapy. The situation involves an adventure into newness which is carried out from a position of confidence: 'good-enough' confidence, that is, learned from experiences of security in danger, difficult passages safely achieved. Thus it concerns the relationship between self and other as this is embodied in symbols of safety and danger involving the contrast between the place I know, which is mine, or at least ours, and every other place, particularly yours – the territory I have conquered and that which I dare not enter. This is the fundamental symbolism of joy and pain, light and darkness, hope and fear, success and failure. Life and death. It is the experience of living emotionally, cognitively and intuitively in two worlds, and the psychological balancing act that this involves – the inevitable experience of being human.

In order to be healed via catharsis, the pity – to use Aristotle's word – that draws us into involvement must be active enough to counter the fear that makes us want to draw back from it. We have seen how pity rises to this challenge most courageously when it is given some kind of cognitive task to do; when the effort of suspending disbelief is enough to give us something to work on, so that our commitment to becoming identified is increased and we are an active part of the dramatic process, rather than a mere spectator. Acceptance of involvement does not simply 'happen', it requires a degree of commitment; in order to share a world, we must play our part in creating it. Catharsis is a process of self-opening in conditions specially prepared for the release of feelings which, in order to be supportable at all, must somehow be shared; in order to be shared, however, they are rendered communicable to the self and to others by the codifying action of structure. It is at this level, that of dramatic structure, that we co-operate in the construction of a shared symbol of meeting. Only in so far as we are willing to let our imaginary forces work are we able to take part in drama at a cathartic level.

Identification with someone else always constitutes a challenge. So, however, does identification with oneself as a personage, a part that one is playing in one's own drama: in other words, self-recognition. These things apply almost equally well to the expository enactment approaches that we were considering earlier. The challenge is the same, as is the threat of danger, of 'death from exposure'. Self-disclosure is always difficult and sometimes extremely painful (see also Jourard, 1964). It would be a mistake to suppose that the oblique approach to personal history, and the immediate awareness of self to which it gives rise, is necessarily less disturbing in its effect than more direct, intentional techniques are. The structure of fiction may cushion us from the initial requirement to revive worlds we have succeeded (more or less) in laying to rest, but it also renders us less prepared for the shock of self-recognition when it arrives, and we discover that it is really ourselves we are talking about. The purpose of the mask is to reveal the face, not to hide it; to reveal it as something new and striking, something that, in a sense, we knew all along but did not need to let ourselves acknowledge to be the case, protected as we were by the objectivity of social roles. With the combination of knowing and not knowing, surprise and recognition, we have arrived at the unique cathartic 'modus operandi', uniting Aeschylus and Caryl Churchill, Oscar Wilde and the Theatre of the Oppressed, Commedia del'Arte and Arthur Miller; indeed everything theatrical from pantomime to black comedy. In all these instances, catharsis happens when we break through the consciousness of role relationship and achieve reciprocity.

This is the origin of the healing power of theatre in all its forms. The only thing that varies is the way that catharsis is achieved and the degree of its intensity. The experience of catharsis occupies a special area of human psychology, one where two very specific kinds of awareness meet and overlap each other. The fact that this does not happen under ordinary circumstances is brought home by their being defined as opposites. When catharsis occurs, the urge to remain separate, with its associated ideas and feelings of vulnerability in the presence of so very much that is not the self, is reconciled with the contradictory human urge to be united with others so that one is no longer lonely, vulnerable and exposed. In the dramatic event, acceptance and rejection fall on each other's necks and weep for the joy of mutual recognition.

This is true for all kinds of happenings that are dramatically 'staged' and which encourage us to share with others our experience of being ourselves. Both expository and exploratory enactment permit a degree of mutuality impossible in situations which do not require the structures of self-presentation to be revealed. The protagonists of psychodrama do not look only at themselves; they see themselves reflected by and revealed in the experience of everybody present at the session. The shock of recognition may not be so great in circumstances where individuals offer themselves freely to be the object of the group's concern, but there is no reason for us to expect the emotional impact of self-disclosure to be less intense. The difference lies in a particular quality of surprise that belongs to the recognition of self in circumstances that are spontaneous and unrehearsed, and where the alternative dramatic world that is being enacted does not appear at first to have any prior claim on the self-awareness of those taking part. As Hamlet says of the weeping actor 'What's Hecuba to him or he to Hecuba?' It is this that disarms us, and manages to do so even when we are by no means in the right frame of mind for sharing confidences with others. This strictly theatrical kind of involvement and identification, involvement in and identification with a character in a play, is found in psychodrama as well, as the other members of the group (Moreno's 'alternative egos') align themselves with the protagonist's own story, putting themselves firmly in his or her shoes. The only difference is that they have come with the definite intention of assisting in a clinical event, while those taking part in more theatrical versions of enactment tend to think more in terms of an imaginative journey or a shared adventure.

'Having killed or abused ourselves, we are able to understand the madness and violence and the many ranges of emotion in Shakespeare's tragedies' (A patient at Broadmoor Special Hospital). Between 1989 and 1991 actors from the Royal Shakespeare Company performed a series of Shakespeare's tragedies at Broadmoor Hospital, a secure psychiatric hospital in the south of England. The story of this experiment in theatre and healing has been recorded in the book edited by Murray Cox *Shakespeare Comes to Broadmoor* (1992). This provided convincing evidence of the truth of his claim that 'the patient dis-covers within therapeutic space as much as he is prepared to tolerate' (1992;128, also 1987). The process is one of disclosure on the patient's part in response to his or her discovery of a truthfulness within the play that resonates with her or his own experience. The theatrical setting for this 'dis-covery' makes it safe enough to bear, so that there is a feeling of emotional and intellectual release, a widening and deepening of awareness that has been painfully, punitively constricted into a space prepared to secure it. Much of what Cox and Theilgaard wrote about in *Mutative Metaphors* receives its theatrical validation in the testimonies recorded here.

> 'When you picked up the skull it really got to me; hit me right in the stomach; I've killed a person and I've done a lot of work on how the relatives must feel, I've played the role of the relatives; but it never

crossed my mind until now that there is a corpse somewhere of the person I killed. I have never thought about the corpse before.'

'He's got the skull on a stick. It made me struggle a bit... He's got that rage all of a sudden. The reality is coming now. And to lighten the load is humour. The door is opened in me'

'I have been to Stratford several times, but the Broadmoor performance was more powerful than any play I have ever seen.' (Cox 1992)

In fact, nearly 20 out of the 80 patients who saw these plays responded to the company's request for feedback, and wrote personally to members of the cast. They had been 'put in touch with things that are far too close' and had lived to tell the tale instead of hiding the knowledge from themselves. Not only they; rehearsing Gertrude, Clare Higgins found the experience of having Hamlet threaten her with his knife 'too close'. It reminded her powerfully of something that had actually happened to her in her own life; 'in the safety of the rehearsal room,' she had decided to use this reaction in her performance, 'because you do feed your personal experience into your work'. On stage, however, the division between what had happened in life to the actress and what was happening to the character completely disappeared; 'here in Broadmoor it seemed that all these worlds came together and fused'. The safety of the rehearsal room had given her the confidence to consider revealing her pain at second hand. Now the spontaneity of the audience's acceptance rendered her sharing totally personal. She met them directly as Clare–Gertrude without any kind of double vision.

This is how she describes the experience:

'I thought: I'm doing this, reliving something that happened to me, within Shakespeare, within the discipline of this production, taking this risk in front of an audience of people who know about it, who may have had it done to them...a bolt of energy hit me in the stomach, and I suddenly felt united with the energy of the people in the room...' (1992; 66)

Clare Higgins's experience and that of other actors in these performances where stories more or less agree with hers, throws a clear light on theatrical catharsis. The joy of acting lies not in display, nor even in self-expression but in the experience of being accepted. Aware of their vulnerability, actors seek the sense of wholeness which lives only in experiences that are genuinely shared. Their vulnerability comes from the fact that they are actually using themselves, their own pains and joys, strengths and weaknesses in order to make the play a world in which the audience will want to live, at least in their imagination. To make oneself this vulnerable is a frightening thing to do. Even to think about it is frightening in the extreme, and can only be done with any confidence 'in the safety of the rehearsal room'. On stage, when the risk of impotence and rejection has been faced, and neither of these things has actually happened, there is still the need to find shelter from exposure 'within Shakespeare', who has provided a character and a dramatic setting to inhabit – both of them a kind of protection against helplessness and 'within the discipline of this production', the painstakingly developed and interiorised ground plan of character and plot.

This is all quite normal. In fact, it is what one might expect to find in any theatrical production anywhere. The factor which made Broadmoor so different was the force of the audience's willingness to take the plays personally. Those on stage were conscious of a quality of acceptance they had never known before. Without the audience's acceptance, of course, there can be no real theatrical happening, because the actors' invitation to share falls on deaf ears. The safety and security that catharsis requires depends only secondarily on structural defences provided by character and plot, and the identity of the play as a play. Before anything else, it is a matter of acceptance, not simply of the play, but of the human truth it contains. Many of the actors involved in the Broadmoor productions were anxious about showing patients on-stage not only experiences they had suffered but actual crimes they had committed. Would they be able to take it? Surely they would feel that they were being got at, and be angrier and more resentful than ever.

Certainly this was not the reaction of most of the audience. Deborah Warner, who directed the Broadmoor *King Lear*, describes 'two girls who had been profoundly moved by the Lear/Cordelia relationship... To play to these two girls alone would be enormous. The world becomes a bigger place.' This kind of involvement 'drew an energy from the audience equal to that of the performers'. The result was 'amazing combustion' (1992: 95). The audience's need for catharsis was equal and probably greater than the actors'. The play provided them with an opportunity for achieving distance from their own wounded identities by making it possible for them to feel for other people – or another person – in a way which they felt safe doing because it was a play. This cathartic trade-off of positive and negative, involvement and defence, reaching out and drawing back, lies at the heart of all theatre-going. Its action is greatly increased because of the presence of so much in the play which the situation of individual patients in the audience rendered painful in the most intensely personal way – so painful that a large part of their personhood was taken up in organising a reaction against it.

Because these plays are violent, they speak directly to people pre-occupied at one level of awareness or other with violence – endured, committed, or both. In this sense, these were the plays for them, because they allowed them to see themselves with the safe clarity that theatre permits, and enjoy a respite from the claustrophobic world of their own private images. The only plays that could help would be those that could equal the outrage. Few people need this theatre more than the mentally disturbed who are also conscious of being criminals. In this case they were grateful of being allowed to share their burdens with others like them in the play. This two way traffic characterises theatre. At Broadmoor it was simply more intense than ever. 'It was interesting what Murray Cox said at the end. The day proved there were not two different worlds, but it was one world.' The patient adds: 'That was the most poignant part of the afternoon, when he said that' (1992:147).

CHAPTER 8

Dramatherapy

Space between?

QUOTE

We have shown how drama provides us with the space and the structures to engage our imagination in the act of identification with ourselves-in-others and others-in-ourselves; and how, properly distanced, this produces a release of emotional tension and the ability to see the world and ourselves in the world in a new way. We have described those aspects of drama which have the potential to heal through the evocation of such a reaction: here, we look at how this is achieved – what Hamlet calls 'the very cunning of the scene'. In our examination of the dramatic structure's intentional use in therapy we shall use various templates to match it against to come closer to an understanding of what actually acts therapeutically, and how it relates to the concepts outlined in previous chapters.

Bloch and Crouch (1985) define the therapeutic factor as 'An element of group therapy that contributes to improvement in a patient's condition and is a function of the actions of the group therapist, the other group members, and the patient himself'. They attempt to make a clear distinction between *therapeutic factors, conditions for change* and *techniques.* The conditions for change are those aspects of the group's structure and procedure without which the therapeutic factors could not come into play. Techniques as they see them are the devices that the therapist uses to facilitate the operation of therapeutic factors. Yalom (1985) (whose ideas about therapeutic factors in psychotherapy were researched and developed by Bloch and Crouch) describes similar factors and conditions, with the caveat that the discriminations that he makes between the factors are arbitrary and that the factors themselves are interdependent. The factors, as outlined by Bloch and Crouch are: insight, learning from interaction, acceptance/cohesiveness, self-disclosure, catharsis, guidance, universality, altruism, vicarious learning and the instillation of hope. This is a slight contraction of Yalom's list which also included corrective experiences and existential factors. Although Yalom's choice of factors is more comprehensive, Bloch and Crouch's work has the advantage of the tightness of their definitions, and their overview of research carried out in relation to the concept of the therapeutic factor.

Let us begin, then, with the conditions for change: those things which are necessary to the operation of dramatherapy, but which are neither techniques nor therapeutic factors. There seems little need to elaborate on the necessity of the co-synchronous physical presence of client and therapist, though we do have a somewhat chastened memory of the group which, when the therapist did not arrive on time, decided to begin the session anyway, with one group member privately fantasising about the possibility of pretending to *be* that particular tardy therapist. The therapeutic space, however, is worthy of much closer inspection. This space is not simply a designated room; it is a special place which must possess, or be invested with particular qualities. We have already described the physical boundaries of the dramatic space, which must in this reckoning include the space *between* the actors and audience, however that is delineated. As we have shown, that space between is essential to drama. While the roles of actor and audience are infinitely more fluid within the context of therapy, the potential for that actual, physical space and for the manipulation of it must be there. You cannot do dramatherapy in a broom cupboard. The material boundaries of the therapeutic space must form a good enough container in that they must exclude (other people, outside distractions) as well as contain (the group, the noise that the group makes...). This may seem trite, but we have experienced groups interrupted by porters wanting to collect furniture...cleaners wanting to collect equipment...ambulance drivers wanting to collect group members...and we have also felt our anxiety levels rise along with the noise levels within the group which sometimes threaten to register on the Richter scale. The space must, therefore, ensure privacy that excludes the outside world and also insulates it from the group.

Dramatic and therapeutic space both have temporal boundaries. When we go to see a play, we know when it will start and roughly when it will finish. The importance of knowing when the performance is going to start is obvious. The awareness of when it will finish is not only useful in terms of booking the post-theatre restaurant table but also in terms of our own security. If the performance is merely bad, at least we know how much longer we have to endure; if our identification with the dramatic image evokes uncomfortable emotions, our awareness of the finiteness of the experience makes it bearable enough to stay on until the end, when, we hope, we will experience some kind of satisfying resolution, or relief. In a very similar way the temporal boundaries of the therapeutic space are important in terms of its ability to contain the emotions of the group.

There are also conceptual boundaries. In therapy the safe space is necessary, not just in terms of privacy, but in terms of what it contains; it is a space which keeps things in as well as keeping them out. It safely contains those emotions which, outside that space, threaten to become dangerous and destructive through their potential capacity to overwhelm the individual. It excludes that which is extraneous to the healing drama. The establishment of this invisible boundary begins with the acknowledgment of the limitations that the group members themselves wish to put into operation; the ground rules of the group. These address the fears that each person brings with him or her to what is often a new experience for them; fear of exposure, of embarrassment, of distress; fear of being seen. The act of making these explicit tends to reduce their power to inhibit, as each person realises that they are not alone in their fear, and the process of identification begins.

The therapist is also a part of these conceptual boundaries; he or she must be seen by the group as someone trustworthy, someone who can contain their distress without either re-suppressing it or being destroyed by it. He or she has a responsibility to open up the therapeutic space, to clarify the border, on one side of which lies the everyday world and on the other lies the world of 'as if'; to make it clear when that border is to be crossed in either direction. Jennings (1994, 7) describes the dramatherapeutic space as 'an actual, concrete or "concrete" place where it is appropriate and safe to establish dramatic reality…' It is also, in her words, a space which 'needs special attention to ritualise its change into the dramatherapeutic space'. Here, she uses the word 'ritualise' advisedly. The opening up and subsequent use and closure of this special space relies on the use of active ritual, in which an individual or group is enabled to move from one state of being to another. We have already mentioned the tripartite structure of ritual and here are concerned with the preliminal stage which moves people away from the everyday world into the world of 'as if'. Grainger believes that the dramatherapeutic space 'should be better at asking questions than producing answers; a space that the group uses and not one that uses the group' (in Jennings, 1994, 7). In the preliminal phase, the group begin to use the space actively and dramatically.

While the creation of a therapeutic space in one way or another is common to all forms of therapy, there are other necessary conditions which are perhaps unique to dramatherapy. We have already described those aspects of our development that initially enable us to engage in dramatic reality. However, that capacity may not be as close to the surface in adulthood as it was for the child. The experience of the original safe space, and the capacity for dramatic play is common to most of us, yet the creative drive which arises out of it and is an integral part of our humanity is often stifled as we mature. A culture whose basis is the creation of wealth has little to invest in creativity (except for the few who can turn their creativity into profit) and much to invest in conformity. Our culture has a major stake in encouraging us to engage in activity which has a price tag attached to it and which has value in economic terms. What price then, what value the realm of the imagination, the plane of 'as if' that most of us were once able to inhabit naturally and easily? The atrophy of the ability to enter into the world of 'as if', where we can test out our actions safely and without repercussion, contributes to a loss of spontaneity and authenticity in our performance in real life. The ability to engage actively in the creation of dramatic reality is a necessary condition for change in the context of dramatherapy; it is a skill that must be reacquired before therapeusis is possible.

A further condition which must be established and maintained is that of aesthetic distance. In Chapter 5 we described in detail the significance of this to the theatrical act. In therapy, the balance between safety and exposure that Jennings (1990) calls the Ritual–Risk paradigm must be kept. The clients must be enabled to come close enough to their own material to be able to engage with it without being overwhelmed by the experience. Aesthetic distance is part of the process of suspension of disbelief as much as the precursor of catharsis. The key here to the maintenance of aesthetic distance is the use of distancing devices, as Scheff (1979) calls them; techniques which are used to achieve a balance between distress and security, within which exploration and ensuing re-evaluation can occur. In the theatre, the audience are overdistanced if they remain unmoved by the drama. They are underdistanced if the drama produces such a degree of emotion that they react as if they were participants in rather than observers of the dramatic act. Here, the necessary space between audience and actors has disappeared. In therapy, the achievement of aesthetic distance is more complex, as group members are both actors and audience. Careful structuring of the experience is vital to preserve the optimal distance between person and person, between person and event. Here, the role of the therapist is crucial: the balance between belief and disbelief, between safety and risk must always be maintained. Participants who are overdistanced from the action will necessarily experience it intellectually; disbelief will remain firmly in place. There will be no true drama and therefore no therapy. If the group is underdistanced, if distress is evoked too acutely, then they will either become stuck in that distress, unable to act, or they will retreat from the action; again, therapeusis will not be possible.

Having established the necessary conditions for change, we must invite the client into the world of 'as if'. At this point, we begin to explore the techniques or structures that bring about therapeusis. The creation of dramatic reality is essential to dramatherapy, and the work of leading writers on drama and theatre, such as Stanislavski, Grotowski and Brook is invaluable as it shows us precisely how this reality is established. We have spoken about the actor who makes the initial welcoming gesture, the offer to the audience to move into a special space where ordinary rules and logic do not apply: where disbelief is temporarily suspended. Who then must make this gesture to the client? Who, indeed makes the original gesture to the neophyte actor? It is the role of the director, as both Stanislavsky (1936) and Grotowski (1991) have pointed out, to create the kind of place where the cast can experiment, can take risks within an overall context of safety. This role also belongs to the therapist, who, as a dramatic artist uses the skills of both director and actor to invite the client into the world of 'as if'; and to set in train the 'willing suspension of disbelief'. In Chapter 3, we described how this occurs within the theatre as an act of collusion between actors and audience. 'Willing' is a key word in the therapeutic act, and herein lies part of the intrinsic safety and power of dramatherapy. In Stanislavski's words:

> 'With this special quality of *if*...nobody obliges you to believe or not believe anything...the secret of the effect of *if* lies first of all in the fact that it does not use fear or force, or make the artist do anything. On the contrary, it reassures him through its honesty, and encourages him to have confidence in a supposed situation... It arouses an inner and real activity, and does this by natural means.'
> (1936, 44)

Here, then, is also the safety, the reassuring quality of therapy. The simple fact that the clients are engaged in dramatic reality rather than everyday reality assures them that they have a control over events which is not necessarily there in the world outside the drama. Given this power, it becomes easier to take the risk of being authentic. In everyday reality, our actions have consequences which we have to live with. In dramatic reality, we are able to act, to witness the results, to disengage from the action and examine it, and then to step back into the arena with increased awareness. As we have already shown, the drive to engage with dramatic reality, the willingness to collude in the dramatic act is a part of our humanity. However, the willingness to engage with 'as if' is not enough by itself. There has to be a way in. As the audience, all that we have to do is purchase our tickets, take our seats and wait for the house lights to dim. The journey into 'as if' that the client must take is not dissimilar to that made by the actor. In order to express and understand ourselves through the medium of drama, we must acquire a dramatic vocabulary. The therapist, as dramatic artist, extends the skills and the experience of drama to the clients, inviting them to claim these skills for themselves.

The initial phase in the process of play development that Jennings describes (1994, 97–101) is that of embodiment; the actual engagement and use of the whole self. This is both a condition for change (in that it is the point of entry into the dramatic system) and a therapeutic factor. We have made reference to the cultural bias against the artistic and the spiritual. It is not only this bias which has tended to limit us. Grotowski describes the split between body and soul which is forced upon us by a culture which is:

> '...characterised by pace, tension, a feeling of doom, the wish to hide our personal motives and the assumption of a variety of roles and masks in life... We like to be 'scientific' by which we mean discursive and cerebral... But we also want to pay tribute to our biological selves... Therefore we play a double game of intellect and instinct, thought and emotion... We suffer most from a lack of totality.' (1991, 211)

Grotowski is by no means the only person to recognise the mind–body split as being a particular malaise of our time. There is evidence of a gradual but definite reaction against the Cartesian style of thought which, through its reductionist approach dissects and pigeonholes our experience of the world, but tends not to complete the cycle by bringing together and creating. The physicist Fritjof Capra (1976) describes the universe as a continuum of interlinked systems, each of which inevitably relates to and is affected by the rest. He initially uses this approach to explore the links between physics and Eastern mysticism, describing in his preface a sudden awareness of 'my whole environment as being engaged in a giant cosmic dance'. In this moment, he integrated his intellectually differentiated perceptions into a fully and actually embodied experience. Later, he develops the theme of holism to challenge the continuing viability of the Cartesian orientation of society. 'Retreating into our minds, we have forgotten how to 'think' with our bodies, how to use them as agents of knowing' (1983, 23). In the endeavour to heal the mind–body split, there is potential for drama, not just as an agent of entertainment, education or individual healing, but as the 'social psycho-therapy' that Grotowski describes:

'Theatre...provides an opportunity for what could be called integration, the discarding of masks, the revealing of the real substance... Here we can see the theatre's therapeutic function for people in our present day civilisation.' (1991, 211)

The primacy that our culture places on a 'reality' determined by the intellect rather than by the whole self has the tendency to produce a kind of dis-embodiment. The body, however, is not merely a vehicle for thoughts and feelings; it is the medium through which they are experienced and expressed. In forgetting this, we risk limiting our own expressive performance in many ways. We are limited not only by the lack of flexibility that comes with encroaching age or unfitness, but also by the patterns of superfluous muscular tension with which we armour ourselves against the world and which inexorably become as fixed and rigid as if we were truly forged out of steel. Psychological distress cannot be separated from physical dis-ease; there is the slowing down of movement and closed posture that is characteristic of depression, the muscular tensions of anxiety, and the chronic patterns of gait, posture and voice that we acquire as we move through life, and which are manifestations of internal processes. The greater part of communication between people is based on what the body is saying rather than the words that are spoken. It follows that a body and voice which are as free from restriction as possible can be used to communicate fluently, and if we wish, honestly. Casson (1994), believes that one of the key therapeutic elements of drama is the fact that it 'engages the whole person; body, voice, imagination, feelings, thoughts in a wholistic, humanist, creative endeavour'. Drama in fact demands this completeness of engagement.

To this end, both Stanislavski and Grotowski advocate the extensive use of physical exercises designed to produce plasticity of movement and of voice. It is worth reading Heilpern's (1989) account of the lengthy and demanding physical preparation that Peter Brook used with his company on their expedition through Africa. These exercises are not carried out in isolation; they do not simply serve as a maintenance routine for the vehicle. Grotowski emphasises the importance of any movement being linked to a clear objective. It must be purposeful – the actor must be sure of why he is doing it. In his *exercises plastiques*, each movement is linked to an image. It is here, at the point where movement becomes purposeful, that the bond is created between actor and character. Having been released from psycho-physiological limitations, the actor is free to explore the physical expression of the character, the set of given circumstances that produce the character's own boundaries.

The use of here and now physical action and awareness are therefore of inestimable importance therapeutically. Individuals who are suffering may become so sunk in their own distress that they develop a kind of defensive numbness to other experiences. To re-enable them to be aware of what is going on within and around them in terms of actual physical sensation is in itself healing. If they are then lifted out of themselves and onto the plane of dramatic reality, they may thereby be sufficiently distanced from their pain to be able to open themselves to other feelings and experiences. If the ability fully to inhabit the here and now is facilitated, then that person is liberated; they can begin to act with spontaneity and immediacy – they can become more authentically themselves. The experience of re-embodiment is often the first experience of the possibility of feeling differently, of moving out of stuckness and into growth. We sometimes suspect that the hardest step for a group or individuals to take is that initial one that moves them out of the chair and into the dramatic space. Once they make that move, the therapeutic journey has begun.

'As if' cannot exist in isolation. The boundaries which demarcate the sphere of dramatic action must be in place. The individual must discover the ability to move freely across these boundaries, yet never lose awareness of where or who he or she is at any one time. A boundary is a container, however, and while it contains nothing it is no more than an empty space, at best a potential. How, then, is this space filled and populated? Brook says 'I can take any empty space and call it a stage. A man walks across this empty space whilst someone else is watching him, and this is all that is needed for an act of theatre to be engaged' (1990, 11). Within the realms of the imagination we can create things which are possibilities in real terms. We can also create things which are not possible within the context of the world as we know it. Through the dramatic act, the actual embodiment of imaginative con-structs through enacting them in front of an audience, an infinity of possibilities can be brought to life, and consequently witnessed and experi-enced. Possibilities are the material with which the imagination works, but they too need a framework to contain them and enable sense and meaning to be made of them in order to gain dramatic reality. For Stanislavski this framework was the clearly envisaged set of given circumstances. He suggests the use of simple questions to move toward the necessary clarity. The actor asks him or herself 'when is this happening? where does it occur? why have these circumstances come about, and how?' The answers to these questions begin to build up a rich and detailed picture that can then be used in the achievement of dramatic reality. In Stanislavski's words:

'If you speak any lines, or do anything, mechanically, without fully realising who you are, where you come from, why, what you want, where you are going and what you will do when you get there, you will be acting without imagination. That time, whether it be short or long, will be unreal, and you will be nothing more than a wound up machine, an automaton.' (1936, 67)

In other words, an awareness of the circumstances out of which a dramatic gesture arises will contribute to the sense of veracity without which the suspension of disbelief cannot be maintained.

In therapy, groups and individuals bring their own given circumstances with them. These are the life events which each has experienced, which have shaped them thus far, and the dynamics of interaction within the group and with the therapist. The given circumstances are also those of character and role; of the sense of 'I am: this is me', embracing as it does the set of attributes, attitudes and behaviours demanded by the individual's self and life-roles. The given circumstances are like a landscape that the client and therapist explore together. This landscape contains not only what has been, but also what could be. One of the therapist's tasks is to aid the client in the process of uncovering these given circumstances and making them explicit. This may take the form of helping people to sketch in the details needed to be able to improvise with confidence, bringing about a sense of competence and mastery. It may be a slow, iterative process; reworking and refining a situation until only the essential aspects remain. Properly envisaged given circum-stances will enable the therapist and the group to create dramatic reality together. If these circumstances are not clarified, even within a seemingly simple dramatic structure, a sense of confusion and stuckness is likely to take hold. This is not the stuckness of resistance, but rather a feeling on the part of the therapist of being unsure of what direction to move in, and on the part of the group of being unsure of what they are being asked to do; in other words, of how to move into 'as if'.

However, it is possible to become swamped by the sheer mass of detail as given circumstances are uncovered. As we have said before, it can be difficult to see the wood for the trees, and this is where theatre has a particular part to play in the clarification of a situation. Stanislavski shows the need for actor and director to identify discrete and significant units of action or narrative which are complete in themselves and which link clearly with the units which precede and follow, acting as wayposts to enable the actor to maintain the right creative direction without being side-tracked by minutiae. Units should flow naturally, like the steps of a dance, so that the dramatic action maintains its impetus and meaning. They should produce a tempo that carries the actors and the audience together through the piece. Each unit in the play's action needs a creative objective to drive it, and here the importance of properly envisaged given circumstances is reinforced. These circumstances provide a stimulus for authentic action precisely because that action is based on a clear objective. Each movement, each word must arise out of an inner intention which renders the action purposeful and therefore real for both actor and spectator. If that objective is clear and understandable, it will produce an action (which naturally encompasses purposeful stillness) and that action will progress the drama.

In order for a sense of reality to exist an objective must, within context, have its own veracity. It must be believable. The actions that have already occurred provide a reality base for an objective, and the action which that objective produces then enriches the reality base for everything that follows. Stanislavski suggests that objectives should be based on verbs; this is one of the most basic principles of objective setting. An objective should be stated in behavioural terms and so produce some kind of action. Grotowski sees this, not dissimilarly, in terms of the actor developing for himself a 'score' that he can follow, based on the body's pattern of reactions, which maps the flow of give and take, of interaction between the members of the cast. The basic elements of the score are 'signs' which themselves are 'purified reaction, a clear impulse', and are tested out by their capacity to evoke belief. As a musical score points out melody, harmony and counterpoint, so in drama, the score provides the actor with his or her objectives, giving each individual a map to follow. As the units and objectives produce a sense of inner truth, or rightness for the actor, he or she can then use them to engage more fully in the 'as if' which is dramatic reality because he believes in what he is doing. His objectives make sense within the context of the whole. His awareness of his actions and reactions, and of the matrix within which they are set contributes actively to the maintenance of that sense of belief.

The use of units and objectives can provide a map to follow in therapy; they give a sense of direction and purpose. In the broadest sense, clients and therapist have an ultimate destination that they are travelling toward – that of health; an actively realised potential for growth. At the most immediate level, a clear dramatic objective frees individuals and groups from a sense of being stuck in what they are doing. It involves a clearing away of dead wood and undergrowth; of finding previously obscured pathways. This objective is not, heaven forbid, an answer that the therapist is steering the clients towards; the 'facipulation' that Heron defines as 'following the client in a way such that the client ends up where the practitioner wants him to be – for the client's own good, of course' (1990, 146). On the contrary, it is the creation of a potential space that can be moved into. What inhabits that space may not be known until it is experienced and explored; here indeed may be dragons. Beyond the dragons, or whatever else is there, is always more terra incognita to be mapped, always space to be moved into. In this way, the framework that the objective gives does not restrict, but actually increases spontaneity and naturalness – in Grotowski's words 'No real spontaneity is possible without a score. It would only be an imitation of spontaneity since you would destroy your spontaneity by chaos' (1991, 192).

We have already mentioned the use of here and now awareness on a fairly simple, physical level. The development of this also needs to be extended to our awareness of others. The client in psychological distress may often find it hard to do just this, and this will naturally affect the quality of his interactions and relationships. The safe space of dramatherapy provides an opportunity to take three kinds of risk: that of seeing others, of seeing ourselves and letting ourselves be seen. If an individual is preoccupied with one aspect of his experience, it is as if he is navigating through a fog. There are treacherous rocks and currents which may be blundered into; there are also safe harbours that may be missed and fellow travellers that are passed by. If the individual can cultivate a greater sensitivity to his own actions and others' reactions, then communication can become a truly mutual and reciprocal process, a game (in both the most serious and playful senses of the word) where the focus can move swiftly or slowly and that can be played as robustly or as tenderly as we wish. 'As if' is the lever, as Stanislavski terms it, that lifts us out of the world of everyday reality and into that of imagination. The given circumstances describe and define that world. But however clearly that world has been envisaged, it cannot actually come to life in dramatic terms until it is physically engaged with. It must be brought out of the imagination and into the shared space between actor and audience. In order to achieve this, Stanislavski suggests that the actor must be able to give effective attention to the world around him and within him. This use of awareness is an active, conscious and deliberate process which not only enables the actor to be authentic, but also to monitor his own authenticity. For many of us, however, there is a tendency to limit ourselves by dwelling on the failures or indeed the successes of our past, or focusing our attention on the future, either with anticipation or fear. In doing that, we cut ourselves off from the ability to experience life as it is happening, here and now. Drama forces us to use our awareness in two directions, inwards and outwards, and demands that we maintain a shifting focus of attention between the two. In therapeutic terms it makes the inward gaze safe enough to become productive and enables an outward awareness that was not previously so available.

This type of awareness is developed by being actively interested in what is going on around us, from the global issues that impinge on our lives to our immediate surroundings and the people who inhabit them. Stanislavski urges his students to seek out and experience not only what is beautiful, but also the less than beautiful: the ordinary and the ugly. There is also the infinitely rich inner world to explore and experience; that world which consists of our thoughts and feelings, ranging from the mountain peaks of passionate emotion to the gentle landscapes of simple physical awareness, the sensation of a chair comfortably supporting the body, the sun warming the skin; awareness of being alive. Once this awareness of the perceived and the inner world is cultivated, it can be exercised in the world of 'as if'. Once the drama begins, this awareness must be extended to the others who inhabit that world. To act, one must truly see the other actors, and the set, and react to them authentically. This is the conscious use of empathy. Awareness must be focused upon what is happening within the boundaries of the dramatic space, rather than directed to the audience. As soon as the actor is seduced into playing to the audience, he becomes in Grotowski's words a 'courtesan'; he loses authenticity. If we, as individuals, also become so seduced, we too lose genuineness – we show what we think others wish to see, rather than sharing the truth – sharing *ourselves*.

Character and role are cornerstones of drama. We have deliberately distinguisheed between the two, as we see them as being discrete yet interpenetrating. The significance of character is fundamental to therapy; its raw material, as it were. It is through our roles, as we have shown, that we present ourselves to others. Role is therefore as crucial to therapy as it is to our social existence. Landy (1993) refers to the concept of role ambivalence; the possibility that there are conflicts within a role, or between roles. He suggests that a balance of role ambivalence is essential; too little ambivalence carries with it the risk of losing dimensionality, whereas too much may lead to confusion. He also links Scheff's concept of aesthetic distance with role by demonstrating how an individual can be over or under-distanced from a role. The risks of becoming typecast, repeating tiny variations on the theme of one role are only too well known to the actor. This is not always a bad thing; after all, many people have built successful careers on a narrow range. In real life, if you are satisfied and content in your own character and comfortable with the way that you meet the demands of the roles that you have acquired, you are unlikely to feel the need to seek therapeutic assistance. In other words; if it isn't broken, don't fix it. But what if you feel stuck in an endless cycle of playing to type in your own life? Here, therapeutic drama gives us the possibility of exploring both the existent character and its dependant roles, and of extending that repertoire. We can see this role development, as Jennings (1994) describes it, in at least two dimensions: depth and breadth. We can experiment with engaging with a role in precisely the way that we usually do, in order to throw into startling relief the patterns that are normally obscured by familiarity. Conversely, by playing a role more fully, or perhaps less intensely than we are used to we can find out just how it feels to play an accustomed role completely differently.

It is enlightening to note how, when the drama takes on a definitely fictional plot, a significant number of people opt for roles that are mischievous, or even wicked. A gleeful kicking over of the traces can be seen. We spend such a lot of our time in life roles that, understandably, require us to play them with kindness, selflessness, understanding that, when the opportunity arises, we choose to be Attila the Hun for a while. And why not! Thus engaging with and exploring our shadow side, we can then re-engage more satisfyingly with our everyday selves. An important factor here is, of course, the safe containment provided by the drama. It is a game, and there are rules; and so the floor does not really run knee deep in blood, nor do the players actually leave behind them a trail of death, destruction and smouldering homesteads. Far from it; the experimentation with being different and the catharsis that arises out of it allow us to re-evaluate ourselves and experience greater personal integration.

Scheff (1979) describes a range of distancing devices; techniques which are used to increase or reduce the distance between audience and dramatic event. This is an observation of what has always been there in theatre, and in showing us how distancing is achieved, he shows us how drama itself works. We feel that these techniques are fundamental to the practice of dramatherapy. As we have shown, in reference to the suspension of disbelief and the induction of catharsis, the *distance between* is a *sine qua non*. The use of these distancing devices, ways of structuring the dramatic experience to maintain optimal distance, is precisely how the dramatherapist operates.

The first of these is the use of immediate, realistic portrayal of an event to decrease distance. The approach is naturalistic; detail in terms of the environment in which the act is set and the characters who inhabit it must be elicited and used. The narrative is placed firmly in the present tense. An accurate re-enactment of the event is created, as if it were happening here and now. This is probably the dramatic form with which we are most familiar. Film and television present us with many examples, from the historical drama with its lovingly recreated period detail to the drama-documentary. Using this approach in therapy, the protagonist would play the part of him or herself. There would be little distance between actor and character. If the event brought onto the therapeutic stage is recreated accurately enough, the client may begin to see patterns emerging that were previously obscured. In life, we are not often fully aware of the given circumstances of the day to day drama in which we are engaged – our attention is focused on the business of getting on with it. In therapy, the given circumstances made explicit act not only as a springboard into 'as if', but also as things in their own right which through being made visible, become more understandable. Once something is made manifest in this way, it gains the potential to be re-worked. Old patterns of being can be transformed into something new, fresh, more creative or useful.

It may well be the case that an accurate representation of given circumstances is too painful or frightening to contemplate. There is not enough distance between the protagonist and the dramatic event to make it safe enough to look at. There is also the risk that the plot will flow along a narrow, almost pre-determined channel, thus missing an infinity of creative possibilities. Anything which renders the dramatic action less immediate, less 'real', increases the dramatic distance and the corresponding level of safety. This shift in the balance between overall safety and overall danger increases the opportunity for risks to be taken and opens up the spectrum of creative and therapeutic potential. Here, we arrive at what is, for us, one of the central concepts of therapeutic drama. When we talk about dramatic distance, we are talking about the space between…between me and you…between you and an object…between him and his inner world. Drama places people and objects within a particular sort of space, in relationship to and with one another. The distance between person and person, person and object, does not have to remain fixed, indeed would not be likely to do so. It can be used both to symbolise and to create emotional distance or proximity, to keep fine tuning the balance of safety and risk, so that therapeutic factors can operate. It is both symbolic in itself, a conceptual space, and at the same time an actual space that can be measured in feet and inches.

Increase or reduction of physical distance produces a corresponding shift in the emotional distance. This distance is both actual and conceptual, in the sense that the physical distance draws attention to the relational. The use of cliché that refers to distance is entirely natural to us: 'too close for comfort'…'I want to keep him at arm's length…' I wouldn't touch it with a barge-pole' and so on. We already know instinctively that in order to deal with things, we must place them at the right distance from us. In his discussion of the use of physical distance, Scheff points out that this distance may be perceived rather than actual. We are all probably familiar with the basics of perspective drawing, where distance is indicated on the flat plane of the drawing surface, which does not of itself have actual depth. Put simply, the larger an object is in comparison with other objects in the drawing, the nearer it seems to be, and conversely to suggest that something is far away, it is drawn small. This trick of perspective can be used dramatically. Jennings (1994, 98–101) shows how drama can also be created in miniature and larger than life. This shift away from life-sized drama is used to modify intensity and safety, again maintaining the balance of aesthetic distance.

When drama is created at miniature level, the apparent distance is increased, enabling the risk to be taken of engaging with something that would not be safe enough at life size. Small objects have a potential combination of power and safety. Objects can be used to create spectograms or minimal sculpts; they can be moved around and given voices, becoming little actors as it were. It is actually very difficult not to project aspects of the self onto inanimate objects used in this way, and the safety lies in their inanimateness. They do not actually possess feelings or thoughts; they do not see or hear or react: through animating them, imbuing them with the constructs of imagination, we can act *through* them. The wooden lion will not become swollen-headed when we identify with his leonine courage, nor will the unused objects feel rejected.[1]

Scheff identifies stylisation as another way of increasing distance. This can include the use of masks, the introduction of mythical or fictional dimensions, disruption of the time-frame and the abstract rendition of events. In our earlier exploration of image and archetype, we referred to the importance of the theatrical image being structured in such a way that it becomes symbolic rather than literal. When we engage the metaphoric aspect of drama, we engineer a shift from 'my story' or 'his story' to 'our story', as what was individual becomes universal. The given circumstances are uncovered; the essential aspects are selected and given a form that not only invites identification but actually makes it almost irresistible. Capra (1989, 69, 80–84), in his exploration of the development of systems theory, reminds us that scientific theory can never be other than an approximate description of reality. The central aspect of systems theory is that of the importance of relationships, and Capra refers to Gregory Bateson's belief that metaphor is the 'language of relationships'. As we have tried to show, metaphor is a basic way in which we attempt to make sense of the world. If we accept that this is so, then it makes good sense to use metaphor openly and honestly as the powerful and beautiful tool that it is. It is just as 'real' as any empirical approach. In the theatrical image, as we have said, metaphor is objectified.

1   cf the discussion of transitional objects, pp 17–19.

In therapy, we use metaphor in this dramatic form to illuminate our understanding of ourselves, by revealing our relationship to ourselves, to others and to the world. In terms of these relationships, nothing on earth stands still. The world as I experience it is not the world that you experience. For both of us, however, there is always the possibility of experiencing it in a new way.

The sources of metaphor for the dramatherapist are infinite. Not only is there the whole field of myth, fiction and dramatic text, there are also the metaphors that individuals and groups themselves produce. Metaphors have a way of emerging unbidden from a particular situation. Perhaps an example would make this point clearer. In a workshop that was designed to enable people to explore ways of dealing with workplace situations, we chose to use the image of the cliff and the sea. We could have taken specific situations and dramatised them, but this would have meant selecting one person's story to the exclusion of others'. We could equally have chosen some textual material to work with. However, the simplicity and richness of this particular image appealed to us. Group members gave physical form, through sound and movement, to these two contrasting entities, and were able to move from being one to being the other, while experiencing both. The sea showed its different faces; wild, rough, calm, playful, nurturing. The cliff did the same; strong, forbidding, protecting, crumbling. The relationship between the two flowed and changed. Individuals experienced these qualities and in doing so acknowledged the ones that felt familiar, but also gave themselves the opportunity to inhabit those that felt different or unusual to them. It became possible, for instance, to move from being the strong, impassive cliff that won't let itself collapse to being the irresponsible, boisterous sea. In making the movement between, it also became apparent that each state of being had an element of choice attached to it. Neither was right or wrong; both were possibilities for each person at any time. Here, the metaphor was brought *to* the group.

An instance of the metaphor arising *from* the group occurred on a hot summer's afternoon, when everyone's mind was focused on heat and thirst. A jug of water was placed in the centre of the floor, and individuals were invited to take some of this water for themselves, and do what they wanted to with it. The improvisations encompassed a huge range of feeling and symbolism, from playfulness to an almost sacramental representation of the preciousness of water. The action became synthesised into one piece which suddenly took on a cyclical structure, showing how water is both transformed and is an agent of transformation. In this moment, the group members were reaching far beyond self awareness and moving towards self actualisation; in one person's words, 'the recognition of the Godly within us all'.

Although the discussions that followed were illuminating, the drama itself was of prime importance. Here, it must be noted that the rationalist tendency to dissect metaphors in order to learn from them is not necessarily useful; drama gives us the opportunity to *experience* and learning arises from and within that experience. The image itself is healing, not our ability to interpret it. This is the case in dramatherapy, and seems to reflect Jung's doctrine that archetypal truth expresses itself as metaphors which lose their force if they are explained away. Healing comes from making contact with human reality at its most basic level by 'staying with the image'.

We would suggest, at this point, that while the therapeutic factors are interdependent, it may be the case that they are, in a way, hierarchical, in that some may need to be in operation in order for others to come into play. The initial factors, those more likely to be experienced earlier on in the therapeutic engagement are those which involve identification with the other. They are brought about by the act of sharing. The creation of dramatic reality by a group of people both demands and produces cohesiveness and acceptance; a degree of trust is necessary for the group to engage, and successful engagement increases trust. Sharing even the smallest part of the self is disclosure, whether it is in the form of personal narrative or in the way that an individual acts and is seen to act within a particular context. Drama highlights the sharing because of the co-presence of actors and audience; as we hope we have demonstrated, the offering of the 'gift of the self' is irresistible. The witnessing of each other is deliberate and acknowledged. Further than this, theatre demands an awareness of the self in relation to others in the creation of dramatic reality that is ultimately altruistic – we give generously of ourselves in the exposition of another's story.

We have seen how a psychological progression from one state to another is expressed in actual physical movement from one position to another, and this is one of the unique properties of drama. When we move, we change our perspective; we can move closer or further away. We alter our point of view. In the liminal phase of dramatherapy, this kind of transition is particularly important, as it brings with it a release of emotional tension. In Chapter 5, we explored this particular aspect of drama; its innate capacity to produce catharsis through aesthetic distance. This function of theatre is central to dramatherapy. Scheff defines catharsis as a discharge of emotional tension which occurs when unresolved emotional distress is reawakened in a properly distanced context, and he believes that catharsis is necessary for therapeutic change to occur. It is important to note Yalom's caveat (1985,

84), supported by Bloch and Crouch, that catharsis in the absence of other therapeutic factors is not enough to elicit lasting change. It is entirely possible to create a dramatic experience that evokes powerful emotional reactions – this is effective theatre. It is not necessarily effective therapy. Catharsis in itself is a powerful experience, but does not of itself produce change. It is the re-evaluation that becomes possible once the previously emotionally charged situation can be seen from a different perspective that enables us at last to move on. Our energies are no longer locked up in suppression and can be expended more fruitfully in expression.

The final group of therapeutic factors is that which encompasses learning; the insight that arises out of our experience. This learning is either direct or vicarious. When insight derives from our dramatic encounter as protagonist it is undeniably direct. However, in the dramatherapeutic milieu it is as likely to occur in a more indirect way; as actors in a universal rather than a personal drama we learn as much from others as from ourselves. This is not the overdistanced engagement of the uninvolved spectator but rather the seren-dipity that is available to us all of seeing and wholly experiencing the self reflected within the other.

We have referred within this book to the tripartite structure of ritual, and have reflected on how the structure of change itself is threefold. We believe that the progression of therapeutic factors also echoes this structure; it can perhaps do no other. The preliminary phase of ritual involves a separation from the everyday world and the willing entry into another. The initial impulse to share, to identify with a special kind of reality, and the experience of that sharing is the necessary precursor to the liminal phase. The conditions whereby it is safe enough to progress from the preliminal to the liminal phase are satisfied if the delicate balance of aesthetic distance is established and maintained. Catharsis and the corrective emotional experience are the central, the liminal phase of therapy; that part of the process in which we pass from one state of being to another. This phase is characterised by confusion, chaos and discomfort. Complete sharing arises out of catharsis, out of the conscious sharing of painful and frightening feelings. If the dramatic balance is sustained, it becomes possible to move on to the final, postliminal phase, where the experience can be evaluated and internalised. Perhaps the most important part of this interiorising is the knowledge of having shared ourselves as fully as we are able, and having been accepted reciprocally in the act of sharing. The tripartite nature of the process is essential. The human impulse is to skip the liminal phase, fraught with unknowing and uneasiness as it is: 'If it were done when 'tis done, then 'twere well It were done quickly...' We all, as Macbeth did, wish to leap from beginning to end, from thane to king, without enduring the space between. And yet even he realised that 'Vaulting ambition...o'erleaps itself...' If we do not risk entering the liminal phase of the therapeutic journey, we can never do other than guess at what might lie on the other side of the threshold.

We have an irresistible urge to understand and master ourselves and our environment. Inevitably, metaphor is the tool that we use to come closer to understanding of any kind. We attempt to simplify our experience; we create models of our universe that are clear enough to hold in our consciousness. Theatre, as a model for humanity and human interaction is perhaps as close as we can come to noumena as opposed to phenomena. Through the theatrical act, the participation in and the witnessing thereof, we can begin to see the wood from the trees, even if at worst it is to see Birnam Wood coming close to Dunsinane. The act of sharing our images and thereby ourselves upon the healing stage gives rise to the therapeutic factors outlined at the beginning of this chapter. Dramatic identification leads to insight and learning. The shared nature of drama produces both cohesiveness and acceptance; as we have said already, that which is personal becomes universal, and that which seems to belong to another is seen also to be part of the self. In allowing ourselves to enter dramatic reality, we reveal ourselves and experience ourselves and others in new and healing ways. Within this safe container we can undergo catharsis and emerge both relieved of old burdens and renewed thereby. As we begin to move away from stuckness and into a new space, hope begins to emerge; change carries within it the seeds of potentiality, and drama is about change. The healing drama enables us to pass from one state of being to another. Having crossed the threshold to the other side we are more sure of ourselves and who we are, not less. We are more able to play our part in the drama of life itself.

CHAPTER 9

Drama and Change

We have explored the relational nature of drama in terms of imaginative identification and the healing processes which arise out of it. Drama is also primarily about change; the movement of individuals from one state of being to another. Through drama, we are able to give form to our experience of change; to have a good look at it and thereby confront our very human fear of it. Change necessarily involves challenging our deepest existential fear; loss of personal identity and integrity – the annihilation of the self. Change is therefore at the very roots of the dramatic act; theatre shows how people are changed by events…or not. Tragedy is the story that unfolds along inevitable lines. It comes about when the character, confronted with the possibility of acting differently, rejects change and thereby chooses or even engineers his or her own destruction.

A point is reached in Anouilh's *Antigone* when Antigone almost chooses to comply with Creon's plea to save herself, to salvage some kind of happiness. Even though the Chorus has made it quite clear to us, the audience, that Antigone will die we still silently urge her to go quietly to her room, to let life go on as before. But no – she turns again to meet her fate as we always knew she would. For her, the change is too terrible to accept; it would diminish her too greatly and death is therefore her choice. Although we weep for her, she retains her integrity. In contrast to this are the characters and choices of Sartre's *In Camera*. Garcin, Inez and Estelle could each have redeemed themselves in life, and chose not to. They are therefore condemned to one another for eternity. And yet potential salvation is still extended to them. As they realise the inevitability of their situation, as the arid plain of their egocentric shallowness stretches out before them Garcin makes the apparently redundant and histrionic gesture of wrestling with the door of the room to which they have been consigned. It opens. Beyond lies the corridor and the unknown. Not one of them dares to cross the threshold.

Their fear of potential annihilation is too great and they would rather continue to collude in their own hell. They reflect back to us our own fear of the destruction of meaning and order, and the consequent onset of chaos. Their room at least holds order, however rigid, and meaning, however bitter; and so they cling to it like children afraid of the encircling darkness beyond the nightlight.

It is likely that ever since there have been adults and children in this world, one of the functions of the adult has been to comfort the child who is afraid of the dark. We have all been that child. Each one of us must recall a time when familiar objects were rendered strange and menacing in the dimness of the bedroom at night; when the boundary between reality and fantasy began to dissolve. On one level, that of logic and reason, we knew that there was not really a monster beneath the bed; only a jumble of toys lay there…but as we became more wakeful and uneasy, keeping very still and quiet…we could almost hear him breathing, beginning to move about in the shadows…reaching out a hairy paw. Looking beneath the bed was not an option for us because the very act of looking might just make the monster real. At last, we would cry out for our parents to come and save us. Antigone herself reminds the Nurse of her own childhood fears, and of how Nurse kept her safe from the 'shadow of the cupboard that used to snarl at me and turn into a dragon on the bed-room wall' (Anouilh 1951, 23).

As parents, we know that our children are not best comforted by simply bringing them more light; this only accomplishes temporary relief. No; we do it by telling the child a story *about* the dark and the monsters that lurk within it. We present the child's fear to him or her in a fictional form that through distancing allows that fear to be experienced and worked through. The child learns that he or she can be in the dark and not be destroyed by it. In just this way, drama demonstrates to all of us the flexibility and resilience of mankind; our ability to change and yet continue to exist.

In Greek myth, the Gorgon destroys anyone who looks directly at her. The only way that the hero Perseus can defeat her is by using the burnished surface of his shield. He is able to look at her through his improvised mirror, so that he can come close enough to her; he is then able to deflect her deadly gaze back onto her, thus turning her to stone. Drama gives us an analogous reflective shield within which we can encounter our fear and survive it. It demonstrates endurable change to us by showing us those very changes that we fear so much through other people, other situations – and we survive alongside them.

It would be wrong, of course, to suppose that our fears are no more than misleading shadows that fade when exposed to the light; but drama begins to teach us how to face them. Its function is also to expose the very real injustices that occur all around us, to force us to question the *status quo*. Drama is an agent of change, not just for the individual, but for society. It does so, in Arthur Miller's words, by 'making man more human'. Inez says to Garcin 'You are – your life and nothing else'. This is so, and yet so much more; we can choose to take personal responsibility for who we are, and the way that we act out our lives. Not one of us, however, lives in isolation from the world; everything is interlinked in some way. We have the potential, therefore, to acknowledge a collective responsibility to ourselves, to each other and to the world. As Tennessee Williams reminds us, 'Men pity and love each other more deeply than they permit themselves to know' (1962). Through showing us the space between, drama shows us where to look for this love. Then it is up to us.

> 'Without safety or daring or trust
> it is not possible for me to go out into the open
> unless the boundaries of my space are well-guarded
> and the wanderer well loved.
> Even the leopard and the panther are easily frightened
> and become vicious
> But they also play and frolic and run and kill with grace and terror'
>
> Miller Mair (1989: 95)

Bibliography

Anouilh, J., 'Antigone', in *Antigone and Eurydice, Two Plays* (London: Methuen, 1951).

Antaki, C. and Lewis, A., *Mental Mirrors* (London: Sage, 1986).

Armstrong, R., *The Affecting Presence* (Urbana: University of Illinois, 1971).

Artaud, A., *The Theatre and Its Double*, trans. M.C. Richards (New York: Grove, 1958); *The Theatre and Its Double*, trans. V. Corti (London: Calder and Boyars, 1970).

Artaud, A., *Oeuvres Complétes* (Paris: Gallimard, 1970).

Aston, E. and Savona, G., *Theatre As Sign-System* (London: Routledge, 1991).

Bandler, R. and Grinder, J., *The Structure of Magic*, (Palo Alto: Science and Behaviour Books, 1975).

Bateson, G., 'A theory of play and fantasy' and 'Epidemiology of a schizophrenic,' in *Steps to an Ecology of Mind* (St. Albans: Paladin, 1973).

Blatner A. and Blatner A., *The Art of Play* (New York: Human Sciences Press, 1988).

Bloch, S. and Crouch, E., *Therapeutic Factors in Group Psychotherapy* (Oxford: Oxford University Press, 1985).

The Book of Common Prayer (Anglican).

Brecht, B., *Die Mutter* (New York: Grove Press, 1965).

Brook,P., *The Shifting Point* (London: Methuen, 1988).

Brook, P., *The Empty Space* (London: Penguin, 1990).

Buber, M., *Pointing the Way* (London: Routledge, 1957).

Buber, M., *Between Man and Man* (London: Collins, 1961).

Buber, M., *I and Thou* (Edinburgh: T. and T. Clarke, 1966).

Burns, C., *Theatricality: A Study of Conventionality in the Theatre and in Social Life* (New York: Harper and Row, 1972).

Butcher S.H., *A Commentary on Aristotle's Poetics* (New York: Dover, 1951).

Capra, F., *The Tao of Physics* (London: Fontana, 1976).

Capra, F., *The Turning Point* (London: Fontana, 1983).

Capra, F., *Uncommon Wisdom* (London: Flamingo, 1989).

Casson, J., 'The Therapeutic Elements in Drama,' (The Newsletter of the British Association of Dramatherapists, Spring, 1994), also 'The Therapeutic Value of Performance (The Newsletter of the British Association of Dramatherapists, Summer, 1995).

Coleridge, S., *Bibliographia Literaria* (1817). (ed) G. Watson (London: Derst Everyman, 1991).

Cooley, C., *Human Nature and Social Order* (New York: Scribner's, 1922).

Cox, M., *Shakespeare Comes to Broadmoor: The Performance of Tragedy in a Secure Psychiatric Hospital* (London: Jessica Kingsley, 1992).

Cox, M. and Theilgaard, A., *Mutative Metaphors in Therapy: The Aeolian Mode* (London: Jessica Kingsley, 1987, 1997).

Cox, M. and Theilgaard, A., *Shakespeare as Prompter: The Amending Imagination and the Therapeutic Process* (London: Jessica Kingsley, 1994).

Crites, S., 'Storytime', in *Narrative Psychology*, Sarbin, T. R. (New York: Praeger, 1986).

Derrida, J., *Writing and Difference*, trans. A. Bass, (London, Routledge, 1978).

Diderot, D., *The Paradox of Acting* (New York: Hill and Wang, 1957).

Douglas, M., *Natural Symbols* (Harmondsworth: Penguin, 1973).

Durkheim, E. and Mauss, M., *Primitive Classification*, trans. R. Needham (London: Routledge, 1963).

Elam, K., *The Semiotics of Theatre and Drama* (London: Routledge, 1988).

Elias, E., The Concept of Dramatic Transference. *Arts in Psychotherapy 19*, 333–346 (1992).

Erikson, E., *Childhood and Society* (Harmondsworth: Penguin, 1965).

Esterson, A., *The Leaves of Spring* (Harmondsworth: Penguin, 1972).

Fairbairn, W.R.D., *Psychoanalytic Sudies of the Personality* (London: Routledge, 1952).

Fairbairn, W.R.D., 'On the Nature and Aims of Psychoanalytic Treatment,' *International Journal of Psychoanalysis* Vol. XXXIV, V (1958).

Flowers, J.V., 'Simulation and Role Playing Methods' in (eds) F.H. Kanfer and A.P. Goldstein *Helping People Change* (Oxford: Pergamon, 1975).

Fontenelle, B. de., *Réflexions sur la Poétique.* 'Je n'ai jamais entendu la purgation des passions par le moyen des passions mêmes' XLV, quoted in F. L. Lucas, *Tragedy* (London: Hogarth Press, 1928).

Fox, J., (ed.), *The Essential Moreno* (New York; Springer, 1987).

Freud, S., *Collected Papers*, vol. 1 (London: Institute of Psychoanalysis, 1925).

Freud, S., Observations on Transference Love, Standard Edition: Vol. 12 (1914) (London: Institute of Psychoanalysis/Hogarth Press, 1975).

Gassel, M., Des Histoires pour Apprendre (Brussels: Editions Savoir pour Etre, 1994).

Gennep, A. Van, The Rites of Passage, trans. M.B. Vizedom and G.L. Caffee (London: Routledge, 1960).

Gersie, A., and King, N., Storymaking in Education and Therapy (London: Jessica Kingsley, 1990).

Goffman, E., 'Encounter', Two Studies in the Sociology of Interaction (Indianapolis: Bobs-Merrill, 1961).

Goffman, E., The Presentation of Self in Everyday Life (Harmondsworth: Penguin, 1990).

Gordon, R., Bridges: Metaphors for Psychic Process (London: Karnac, 1992).

Grainger, R., The Social Symbolism of Grief and Mourning (London: Jessica Kingsley Publishers, 1997).

Grainger, R., Presenting Drama in Church (London: Epworth, 1985).

Grainger, R., The Message of the Rite (Cambridge Lutterworth, 1988).

Grainger, R., Drama and Healing (London: Jessica Kingsley, 1990).

Grossvogel, D., The Blasphemers (Ithaca, NJ: Cornell University Press, 1962).

Grotowski, J., Towards a Poor Theatre (London: Methuen, 1991).

Halmos, P., (ed.) 'Papers on the teaching of personality development', The Sociological Review Monographs, I, (Keele University: 1958).

Halmos, P., The Faith of the Counsellors, (London: Constable, 1965).

Hamilton, M., 'Knowledge and Communication in Children', in C. Antaki and A. Lewis, (eds.), Mental Mirrors (London: Sage, 1986).

Heilpern, J., The Conference of the Birds (London: Methuen, 1989).

Heron, J., Helping the Client (London: Sage, 1990).

Hillman, J., Revisioning Psychology (New York: Harper, 1972).

Hillman, J., Archetypal Psychology, (Dallas: Spring Publishers, 1983a)

Hillman, J., Healing Fiction (New York: Station Hill, 1983b).

Jennings, S., Dramatherapy with Families, Groups and Individuals: Waiting in the Wings (London: Jessica Kingsley, 1990).

Jennings, S. et al. The Handbook of Dramatherapy (London: Routledge, 1994).

Jennings, S., in A. Gersie (ed) Dramatic Approaches to Brief Therapy (London: Jessica Kingsley, 1996).

Jones, P., 'Dramatherapy: Five Core Processes' Dramatherapy, XIV, 1 (1991).

Jourard, S., The Transparent Self (New York: Van Nostrand, 1964).

Jung, C.G., *Psychology and Religion* (New Haven: Yale University Press, 1938).

Jung, C. G., *Collected Works*, Vol. 6, (Trans. R.F.C. Hull, Bollingen Series XX, Princeton: Princeton University Press, 1953).

Jung, C.G., *Analytical Psychology* (London: Routledge, 1968).

Kanfer, F.H., and Goldstein, A.P., (eds), *Helping People Change* (Oxford: Pergamon, 1975).

Keen, E., 'Paranormal and Cataclysmic Narratives', in T.R. Sarbin, *Narrative Psychology* (New York: Praeger, 1986).

Kelly, G., *The Psychology of Personal Constructs*, vol. 1 (New York: Norton, 1955).

Kielhofner, G., (ed) *A Model of Human Occupation* (Baltimore: Williams and Wilkins, 1985).

Knight, W., *The Principles of Shakespearian Production* (Harmondsworth: Penguin, 1936).

Klein, M., 'Notes on some schizoid mechanisms', *International Journal of Psycho-Analysis* 27 (III) (1946).

Klein, M., *Love, Guilt and Reparation*, (London: Virago, 1988).

Lacan, J., *Écrits: A Selection*, trans. A. Sheridan (New York: Norton, 1977).

Landy, R.J., *Persona and Performance* (London: Jessica Kingsley, 1993).

Levinas, E., *Totality and Infinity* (Pittsburgh: Duquesne University Press, 1969).

Lewis, G., *The Day of Shining Red* (Cambridge: University Press, 1980).

Lucas, F.L., *Tragedy* (London: Hogarth Press, 1928).

Lucretius, *De Rerum* (On the Nature of Things), Trans. M. Ferguson Smith (London: Sphere, 1969).

Mair, M., 'The Community of Self', in D. Bannister, (ed.), *New Perspectives in Personal Construct Theory* (London; Academic Press, 1977).

Mair, M., *Between Psychology and Psychotherapy: a Poetics of Experience* (London: Routledge, 1989).

Maslow, A., *Towards a Psychology of Being* (Princeton: Van Nostrand, 1962).

May, R., *The Courage to Create* (London: Collins, 1975).

McDougall, J., *Theatres of the Mind* (London: Free Association Books, 1986).

McGuire, W. and Hull R.F.C., *C.J. Jung Speaking* (London: Thames and Hudson, 1978).

Mead, G.H., *Mind, Self and Society* (Chicago: University Press, 1967).

Merleau-Ponty, M., *The Phenomenology of Perception* (trans. C. Smith), (London: Tavistock, 1962), XVI.

Moras, K. and Strupp, H.H., 'Pre-Therapy Interpersonal Relationships: Patients' Alliance and Outcome in Brief Therapy,' *Archives of General Psychiatry* 39 (1982).

Moreno, J.L., 'Psychodrama' (New York: Beacon House, 1959), in J. Fox (ed.) *The Essential Moreno*, (New York: Springer, 1987).

Moreno, J., 'Sociometry' (1937), in J. Fox (ed.) *The Essential Moreno* (New York: Springer, 1987).

Pepper, S., *World Hypotheses* (Berkeley: University of California, 1942).

Perls, F., *The Gestalt Approach, Eyewitness to Therapy* (Palo Alto: Science and Behaviour Books, 1973).

Perls, F.S., Hefferstone, R.F. and Goodman, P., *Gestalt Therapy* (Harmondsworth: Penguin, 1973).

Polster, I. and M., *Gestalt Therapy Integrated*, quoted in R. Bandler and J. Grinder, *The Structure of Magic*, (Palo Alto: Science and Behaviour Books, 1975).

Raphael, D.D., *The Paradox of Tragedy* (London: Allen and Unwin, 1960).

Rogers, C., *Client-Centred Therapy* (London: Arnold, 1976).

Russell, B., *History of Western Philosophy* (London, Allen and Unwin, 1961).

Sarbin, T.R., *Narrative Psychology* (New York: Praeger, 1986).

Sartre, J-P., 'In Camera', in *Three European Plays* (Harmondsworth: Penguin, 1958).

Scheff, T.J., *Catharsis in Healing, Ritual and Drama* (Berkeley: University of California Press, 1979).

Semmes, J., 'Hemispheric Specialization: A Possible Clue to Mechanism' *Neuropsychologia, 6,* 11:26 (1968).

Shapiro, L.N., 'Has the Scope of Psychoanalysis Changed,' *Psychiatry Update: American Association Annual Review* Vol 2, Washington D.C., American Psychiatric Press (1983).

Shakespeare, W., *Hamlet Prince of Denmark.*

Shakespeare, W., *Julius Caesar.*

Shakespeare, W., *Macbeth.*

Shakespeare, W., *Sonnet XVIII.*

Stanislavski, Constantin, *An Actor Prepares* (New York: Theatre Arts, 1936).

Steiner, G., *Language and Silence* (Harmondsworth: Penguin, 1969).

Turner, V., *The Ritual Process*, (Harmondsworth: Penguin, 1974).

Unamuno, M., *Tragic Sense of Life*, trans. M. Ferguson Smith (London: Sphere, 1969).

Watkins, E., 'Transference Phenomena in the Counselling Situation', *Personnel and Guidance Journal*, 62 (1983).

Willett, J., *The Theatre of Bertolt Brecht* (London: Methuen, 1960).

Williams, T., Preface to 'The Rose Tattoo', *Five Plays* (London: Secker and Warburg, 1962).

Wilshire, B., *Role Playing and Identity* (Indiana University Press, 1982).

Winn, L., *Post-Traumatic Stress Disorder* (London: Jessica Kingsley, 1994).

Winnicott, D.W., *Playing and Reality* (London: Tavistock, 1971).

Winnicot, D.W., *Human Nature* (London: Free Association Books, 1988).

Yalom, I.D., *The Theory and Practice of Group Psychotherapy* (New York: Basic Books, 1985).

Subject Index